TELL ME A
STORY

Lisa Suhay

PARACLETE PRESS
BREWSTER, MASSACHUSETTS

Library of Congress Cataloging–in–Publication Data

Suhay, Lisa, 1965–
    Tell me a story / Lisa Suhay.
        p. cm.
    ISBN 1-55725-247-5 (hc)
    1. Fables, American. I. Title.

PS3569.U2533 T45 2000
813'.54--dc21

99-057509

Photographs © 1999 by Steven M. Falk
Original artwork © 2000 by Calligraphy Guild of
The Community of Jesus, Inc.

10 9 8 7 6 5 4 3 2

Brewster, Massachusetts
www.paracletepress.com

Printed in the United States of America.

Dedication

The characters and stories in this volume
were inspired by everyday life. I have been fortunate
that my life has contained so many amazing people
and experiences. When you are given such a
great gift it is only right to say thanks.

Thank you to:
My sons for giving the characters innocence and joy.
My husband for giving them passion and depth.
My mother for sharing her strength.
My brother for hope.
To Fern and Ed for giving them the power
that comes from being nurtured.
I thank Heaven for all of them.

I would like to dedicate "The Crane Stories" to
Betty Bruno of Goodland, Florida,
who flew from us but introduced me to
the crane before she went.

Table of Contents

Foreword

Once upon a time, there was a man who sought a way to reach others with words. In his quest to touch people's lives for his Master, he set out in pursuit of the words his subscribers would find so inviting to read that, until they finished, they would be unaware they had learned something of great value. Forlorn, the editor could find precious few who would spin the creative verbal webs he sought.

Then one day, an enchanting parable came to him via the great expanse we have come to call cyberspace. And lo, many were touched, as was the man himself. Then came another, and another, and soon the editor's daily postings were graced with the charming allegories he had been seeking for lo these many years.

From the first day Lisa Suhay sent me her story "The Diamond of Hope" for Daily Wisdom, I knew that I would soon see her name in print. Now, only about a year later, the volume you hold is proof that her imaginative tales carry the universal charm that was evident from her first sentence, as well as the lifelong treasures that can somehow be conveyed well only through a great story.

Lisa once told me she hoped perhaps to see her works published in children's literature. I thought it a little sad that we (alleged) adults would thereby be deprived of the fine verbal journeys she so consistently weaves. The themes presented between these covers are far from limited to children, yet they have a way of transporting one back to a childlike innocence while driving home grownup lessons with style. Read them to your children and grandchildren, by all means, but read them for yourself. You won't be disappointed.

From the quixotic endeavors of a benevolent dolphin, to the change of heart of a greedy magpie, to the neighborly support of a twisted tree, your own excursions through these pages can help you keep alive the truths that kindness still begets kindness, that helping another with a problem can diminish our own, and that whoever truly wants to, will see the crane's home in the sky.

Jesus himself knew that his hearers could best absorb his teachings as parables. He knows that, given the choice between plot and pontification, we will often hearken to the entertaining story over the sermonized soliloquy. So as you read, enjoy, and learn from the creative fables beyond this page, prepare to be thoroughly entertained as you find lessons of wit, contemplation, and perhaps, Lord willing, eternal value.

Warren Kramer
Editor, Daily Wisdom Online Devotional
Muskegon, Michigan

Preface

How does a writer go from newspapers and the harsh realities of life to the creation of gentle parables and fables for the modern world? It often makes me wonder myself, but the truth is that one day I decided to relinquish my iron grip on reality and listen to what the world had to say for itself.

I was angry, worried and sad in many ways.

The mother of two young boys, ages five and four with a third on the way, I was constantly finding ways to explain life's difficulties to my children. I would take their real life problems and assign the people involved an animal character. Then I would weave a tale of how the problem was solved.

One night, while I sat brooding over a problem of my own, I said a little prayer and asked for a solution. What I really asked for was a way to let go of my anger or hurt or whatever the fear of the day was.

Because I think better with a keyboard at my fingertips I sat down at the computer and tried to clear away my feelings and approach the problem through the eyes of a frog, a dog or bird, as I did for the boys. The result is contained in the pages of this book.

I would love to take credit for the result, but in truth I don't think I am really clever enough or compassionate enough to have come up with all these answers on my own. Call it the Spirit or some universal energy that worked its way through my fingers and onto the printed page, but the result surprised me. As they say, I didn't know I had it in me.

The real truth is that I think "it" is in all of us. All we have to do is look at ourselves through the eyes of a frog to leap for joy, a bird to soar, or a cricket to sing the music that is written on our souls.

Lisa Suhay

IN THE
BEGINNING

The Diamond of Hope

nce there lived a man whose business it was to tend precious stones. He was a jeweler of good repute but little sense.

It came to pass that a woman went to his shop and handed him a pouch containing a fabulous diamond known as the Diamond of Hope.

The jeweler was thrilled to be entrusted with the precious stone. It had a certain luster and spark not often seen. He thanked the woman and promised to give it the utmost care.

Unfortunately, the stone weighed heavily on his mind. The gem appeared a bit dusty, but he dared not polish it. He was afraid that underneath he would find a flaw.

Also, he thought, how could it be that the woman had chosen him? He had seen gems such as this but knew one would never cross his path. Something must be amiss.

The next day the man showed the stone to his colleagues. They were skeptical. "How could this be so precious a stone?" asked one. "It is the wrong size. It is too small."

"It is flawed," cried another, rubbing hard with a rag. "Look closely. See, there, the color is too yellow in one spot."

3

Though the jeweler argued that color, size, and even flaws were not necessarily indications of a lack of worthiness, the others urged him to throw the stone away.

"It is not of the worth you had thought," said a colleague. "However, bandits might not see the flaws and may kill you merely to possess it. It is not worth the risk."

Now both the man and his colleagues were in a dither over the rock.

At length they chose to seek out the woman and return it to her. After all, it was she who had placed them all in such danger over a mere hunk of mineral.

After the stone was gone, the jewelers toasted their wisdom and good fortune.

The stone was taken to another jeweler who examined it and found it to be of great value and charm. Placed in its new setting, it shone with even greater luster and brought joy to all who beheld it.

As the years passed, the first jeweler found he had fewer and fewer customers, for the story of his folly had spread and his judgment was no longer valued.

Birch Finds Its Roots

In the beginning there was a wondrous great tree that grew in the center of a wide and open field. Its branches spread out and gave shade to the ground beneath. Its trunk was white as snow, its leaves of the finest gold.

In the spring it flowered and gave off a scent that could make dreams into reality and reality into dreams.

Seasons changed and in time the Great Tree would produce many seeds. Some would drop upon the earth, others would blow across the field; still others would be carried by birds and field mice to far off lands. Some would perish. Most would grow and drop seeds of their own.

Every seed was unique in all the world. Each tree that grew would be a variation of the Great Tree, but none could duplicate it precisely.

One tree grew in rocky soil and chose to lean toward the shade rather than the sun. In the shade it became bent and gnarled.

Having such obvious flaws made the tree angry.

"All of my siblings are perfect and straight," the young tree complained to the Great Tree. "I hate them. I will send my roots to choke them out. I will stretch my branches to shade them whenever I can."

The Great Tree sighed. "My child," it said. "You are unique in all the world. You are my child and I love you. I beg you, do not harm the others. Find beauty in your strangeness. Glory in your twists and bends."

The Dark Tree could not find joy in its lot in life and it went ahead and did the harm it had promised. Many trees suffered.

Nature is far-seeing, and even the most bent and gnarled tree can produce seeds and continue the cycle of life. So it was for the Dark Tree. Not being as large and healthy as many of the others, it only produced three seeds. All landed in the sun. All took to the soil and grew.

When they were just seedlings, they looked across the field at their sire and worried.

"It is so dark and bent," said the first seedling. "What if we grow as dark and do great harm? I shall close my eyes and never look at it or anything that reminds me of its terrible ways."

"I shall never be like that," said the second. "I would rather wither and die than be like that one. I shall only look away from it, and so I will grow straight and tall and perfect. I shall pretend it does not exist."

The third seedling thought hard about this decision. "I shall look at it and never away, for I must always be reminded of where I might go wrong."

They all grew up.

The first tree kept its eyes closed and could never tell where the sun was coming from. It sent out runners and roots in search of direction. By accident it choked several other trees. The tree became so confused that it began to bend toward the earth instead of the sky.

It cried in despair. It wept so hard that its leaves became tears flowing down its long thin arms. The weeping willow was a lonely tree.

The second tree found that the only way to keep from being reminded of the Dark Tree was to look straight up at the sky. It never cried. It held everything inside. It built thick walls around its trunk and arms. The fear it could not contain grew out of these walls in long, thin, sharp spikes.

Anyone going too near cactus would be speared. It was self-sufficient but too thorny for company.

Through it all, the Great Tree looked on and grew sad. "Oh, my poor suffering children," it said. "Can none of you find your way in this world?"

The third tree had spent its life looking upon the Dark Tree. It had come to know all its many facets. It saw the straight and the bent. It watched other trees and felt sad and ashamed.

The third tree became thin and frail, a mix of papery white bark and black knots. Its leaves were green on top and silver beneath. It knew it would not live so long as the other trees, and it yearned for a way to reconcile its fears and hopes.

One day the birch, for that is what it had become, stood looking at the Dark Tree. The Dark Tree waved at it.

In all the years, this had never happened. Then the birch heard the Dark Tree's voice carried on the wind. "You have some of my coloring in you my child," the Dark Tree said. "Parts of you are dark. You will carry on my name. Sink your roots deeper to hold you down and then choke off your neighbors. Clear a path for yourself."

Hearing this, the Great Tree shook. Though there was no wind that day, the golden leaves stirred and waved.

"Little birch, hear me now," the Great Tree said in a rich flowing voice. "You have spent your life looking at your sire. Look up now and see me instead. I came before the Dark Tree that bore you."

"You are a part of me as well. Your roots run back to me," the Great Tree said. "You make the choice as to how you will grow. Straight or bent, happy or sad, pointed or smooth."

The Dark Tree would have none of this. It wanted a partner, and it would not have this young one snatched away. It had waited too long for the triumph.

"Do not look up, birch," the Dark Tree said. "You are not strong enough. You will snap. You will shatter. Keep only me in your sights and all will be as it should be."

The Great Tree knew that the little tree was frightened. It could see it shuddering. "Be not afraid," the Great Tree called out. "I know what is within you, for it came from me."

With those words the Great Tree released its golden leaves into the air. Instead of raining to the ground, they floated high in the air. Like a million golden butterflies they fluttered across the field and came to fill the air around the birch.

The golden leaves gave off a scent that could make dreams into reality and reality into dreams. They warmed the little tree, and a light that seemed to shine from them soaked into its bark. Then they fluttered back to the great one and stood back on its branches.

"Rise, little one," the voice said. "Look up at me and bend. You will not break now."

So the little birch tree looked up at the Great Tree and saw it in all its glory. The little tree saw the white bark and knew it was a variation of the Great Tree.

"You have both your sire's darkness and my light upon you," the Great Tree said. "It is up to you to decide which you will favor."

The little birch reached and waved to the Great Tree. It swayed back and forth in celebration of this new discovery.

"I will look up to you," it said in a shivery little voice that was all its own. "I will bend to you, reach for you, and remember always that I come from you. You are my real parent. Never again will I fix my gaze only on the dark now that I have seen your golden light."

The leaves of the Great Tree shone with pride. While the birch was only one more little tree among forests of trees, it was a start. With an open heart and a little guidance, seedlings could grow into great trees.

Sleeper's Awakening

earning to tie his shoes had not been difficult for Sleeper possum. This was because every time his shoes came undone, his older brother, Rushin, would tie them for him.

"Rush," their mother would call. "Let him do it for himself. He will never learn if you do it for him."

"Yes, Ma," Rush would answer. Of course he had no intention of paying her any mind because he was sure she was wrong.

He had let Sleeper try for himself and it had taken an eternity. In the end he had got it all wrong and so Rushin ended up tying them. It was always easier to do it himself.

Besides, it made him feel so good to be the one Sleeper came to for help. It made him feel big and important. It made him feel like a benefactor to his little brother. Rushin was always praised for his good works.

"Such a good one," they would say, and pat him on the head. "See how he cares for his little brother."

So it went from the tying of shoes to making breakfast and then to talking and reading. Sleeper would start to struggle along to try some new task and Rushin would roll his eyes and then come to the rescue.

"No, no, no." He would sigh. "Here, let me show you."

It wasn't far from "Let me show you," to "Here, let me do it." Then, of course, it was just a stroll over to, "Don't bother! You'll never get it right."

Sleeper was an easy-going possum. He saw how happy it made Rushin to do things for him, so he let his brother continue. He stopped tying and cooking and speaking. He very nearly stopped thinking.

The thinking crisis took place one day when they were preparing the little boat that Rushin had made for her maiden voyage. They were going to sail across the big bay and out into the ocean.

For months on end Sleeper had hung by his tail in a nearby tree and watched his brother craft the boat. Sleeper was an excellent observer. He saw how his brother framed the hull, set the sides, and caulked the gaps with thick cotton. He noted how Rushin stepped the mast and rigged the running lines.

Sleeper saw the beauty and the flaws. He knew that, while the craft was beautiful in line, it was not sturdy enough to go on the open sea. Anyone else would have mentioned this before the launching day, but Sleeper was not anyone else. It had been so long since he had done anything for himself that he had lost faith in his own judgment.

He looked at the boat and thought, "If I were a smart possum I would say that this boat will fail its master in the first hard wind."

Then he shook his head and tugged hard at his whiskers. "No," he thought. "I cannot be right. Rushin is the really useful possum. He can do anything. He will only tell me I am mistaken."

Though Sleeper was an easy-going sort, he did not like it when his brother chided him or made fun of his clumsy ways.

It never occurred to him that he would not be clumsy if he practiced his tasks himself. He had long forgotten that he was not taking action in order to make his brother happy.

Now he took no action because he was afraid of failing. He needed his big brother's approval so much that now he asked his permission to eat and sleep.

Rushin had gone from feeling big and grand to feeling put-upon and irritated. He still tied his brother's shoes and made his breakfast and spoke for him. Only now it was all done in a martyred tone.

"You should thank Heaven that you have me here to help you," Rushin would say. "I don't know how you would ever make it on your own. Of course helping you is my life and I am glad to do it."

Rushin had taken to letting out great, gusty sighs each time he saw his brother about to try at a new task. He rolled his eyes and shook his head and twirled his whiskers knowingly. By the time Rushin's performance was over, Sleeper would lower his head and turn the task over to his elder sibling.

"He really is hopeless," Rushin would tell people. "It is exhausting trying to care for him and still find time for myself."

So it had been until the day of the launching. Rushin had planned and packed and preened over his upcoming success. He made sure Sleeper's bags were properly packed and had refolded his brother's shirts just so. He made sure Sleeper had only the simplest of tasks for the event. Sleeper was to cast off the lines.

Sleeper was a nervous wreck. He had practiced casting off the lines over and over again. The only problem was that he was not sure that he should do it when the time came. He had nightmares about the boat foundering.

He had even gone so far as to take a book out of his brother's collection and read it in bed. Oh, yes, Sleeper could read. He had taught himself, but tried hard not to let his brother know. He was sure that he was not very good at it.

Still, the book seemed to confirm his worst fears. The lumber his brother had used was far too thin. It looked handsome, but was not strong.

Now it was time to face the day and his brother.

"Sleeper," Rushin hissed in his ear. "You are day-dreaming again. It is time to cast the lines."

All eyes were on Sleeper as he gripped the thick hemp in his paws. He looked from his brother to the animals gathered on the dock. Sleeper cast the first line and the crowd cheered. His brother nodded for him to cast the second line. Sleeper tossed it to the crowd.

When it came time to release the third and final line, his paws locked on it in a death grip.

"Let it go," Rushin shrieked. "What is wrong with you?"

Instead of letting go, Sleeper made his decision and

made the other two lines fast again. Then he took a deep breath and faced his brother.

Nearly apoplectic with frustration, Rushin charged past his brother, knocking him to the deck. He would loose the lines himself. He always had to everything, why should today be any different?

"The boat will sink brother," Sleeper croaked out, for his mouth had gone dry with fear. "You cannot sail her. She is not sound."

Rushin dropped the line as if it had been a live snake and wheeled around. "You have no idea what you are talking about," he fumed. "You cannot even tie your own shoes, much less judge my work."

Sleeper looked down at his shoes. Perhaps he had been wrong to speak out. Despite the anger and contempt he saw on his brother's face, he knew that his brother loved him. He loved Rushin and saving him was worth the wrath that would come as a result of this moment.

Taking his time and choosing his words carefully, Sleeper explained his concerns about the boat. He even took the book from his sea pack to illustrate his findings. Then he took a step off the boat and onto the dock. He waited for the worst to happen.

Rushin did not know what struck him more fiercely, the fact that he had not seen the boat's flaws, or that he had been so blind to his brother's attributes. A parade of emotions marched through his mind. First was anger, followed by embarrassment, and guilt, and then came pride.

The pride was in his little brother.

"You taught yourself to read," he said softly.

"Yes, but I am sure I don't do it so well as you," Sleeper said quickly.

Rushin stepped off the boat and onto the dock beside his brother. He put his arm around him. "I think you are better at it than I," he said. "You read it and put the knowledge to use. I am sorry that I held you back."

"I let you do the holding," he answered. "I am as much to blame."

"Well, my friends," said Rushin. "My brother has saved the day. All these years I have taken matters out of his hands. Today I find that in his hands I would gladly place my life."

Looking solemnly at his brother Rushin said, "I hope that my little brother will never play possum again. It is far too dangerous a game."

Chandra's Change

ooking down at the branches of the tree, one could see many shades and colors. What could not be seen was the chameleon, perched on a branch and sitting perfectly still.

"I will blend. I will blend," she thought. In her mind she repeated, "One with the branch. One with the tree. Sit very still and they won't see me."

So it was that Chandra the chameleon spent her days and nights. When she did move, it was always a calculated risk. Her movements were slow and deliberate. One long toe at a time would uncurl from the branch, and then she would flow to the next spot on the tree and freeze.

To blend in with the tree meant safety to Chandra. Being different or standing out could mean death. A bird or snake or other animal could spot her too easily and consume her. So her colors changed.

To a chameleon, it was imperative to feel oneness with the surroundings. She had not only to think of the color green, but to imagine how green must feel in order to assume its hue.

"Green is alive," she thought. "Green is unripe. New. Fresh. Honest is green." And so she would be green.

16

"Yellow," she thought. "Yellow is joy. Bright. Sunny. Warm is yellow." And so she would become yellow.

Moment to moment Chandra would move and freeze and change to fit her tree.

It was an oppressive afternoon in the rainforest where her tree grew. The leaves of the canopy were still, for they lacked a breeze to stir them. Birds called. Moisture dripped to the ground.

Chandra peered from her branch. One eye looked up, the other down. It all happened so quickly that later she would be tempted to believe that she had imagined what happened.

Two apes, swinging from vine to vine, landed right in front of her. One was in a terrible state. She was puffing and shrieking and the larger, a male, was coiled to attack. Chandra recognized him as Tarak, king of the apes.

"Please, spare me," the lady ape begged. "Let me go."

Tarak beat her with a stout branch he held. "I do what I please, little Miss Nan. You have criticized my leadership long enough. Now you will learn a lesson. If you ever speak against me again, I will beat you till you speak no more."

When he was through, he swung away, leaving Miss Nan behind. Chandra could hear her crying but did not move. After all, what could she do to help? If she moved she might well be eaten. Did apes eat chameleons? Better safe than sorry.

By and by Miss Nan stopped her crying and began to lick her wounds.

"I am sorry you had to witness that," she said in Chandra's direction. "I should not have begged mercy from such as him."

Chandra slowly moved her eyes to try to see to whom the ape was speaking. She saw no one.

"I am speaking to you, chameleon," she said. "Yes, I see you. That is my problem. I see too much sometimes, and then I must speak out about it."

When Chandra did not move or respond, the ape said, "Do not be afraid. I will not harm you."

"You should not do things to anger others," Chandra was surprised to hear herself say. "You should stay very still as I do. You should stay silent."

The ape looked at Chandra for a long, measuring moment.

"Perhaps what you say is true," she said. "I saw that ape doing harm to others. He takes advantage of the weak and the poor and the elderly. His cruelty is legend. To remain silent would have made me feel a party to his actions. That is not in my nature."

Chandra was confused. "Did not your people say, 'See no evil, hear no evil, and speak no evil?' You should close your eyes, cover your ears, and stay silent. That is the prudent thing to do."

In spite of her wounds Nan laughed. "A fine picture I would make, sitting in that manner."

"Your speaking up did not help anyone," Chandra argued. "All it did was bring you pain."

The ape sighed. "There is truth in what you say. Unfortunately, I cannot do as you do. I must return to my fellows and do my best to stop that evil one in any small way I am able. I will return to free his slaves and tend the sick."

"Come with me," she urged. "I need someone who can blend in as you do. Watch my back. You could sit and watch out for his coming and warn me."

For the first time in her life Chandra was in a quandary over what to do. She desperately wanted to follow Miss Nan and see that she remained well. Of course Chandra was terribly afraid and unsure.

"Your cause seems just," Chandra said. "I am only a tiny creature and I could not be a big help."

Nan smiled. "It is the size of the ideals, not the being, that makes one great," she said. "Come and ride on my back."

With the quickest motions she had ever made, Chandra leaped onto Nan's back and thought deep, brown thoughts.

To Chandra, the ride on Nan's back as she swung from tree to tree was the most thrilling time of her young life. Then they landed in the big tree of exile and she felt a deep and abiding sadness.

All around were refugees from the evil king's trees. Tiny faces of the little ones, their eyes dark with fear, peered from behind their mothers. Elders, battered and tired, hunkered in corners. All the young male apes were absent, conscripts in the king's guard.

Miss Nan worked quickly. She bandaged some, rocked and consoled others. Mostly she talked. She told them of staying together and not losing hope. She promised them a better life. She prepared them to flee to freedom.

Chandra had not forgotten her job and when she saw the shadow of the king swinging toward the tree she warned Nan by tugging on her fur.

Nan grabbed a sharp stick and began to fight against Tarak.

Chandra tried to close her eyes and think "Brown! Brown! Brown." It was no use. She looked up at Tarak and turned white with fear.

One moment Tarak was fighting the meddlesome little female ape and in the next he saw a vision. A white creature had reared up on Miss Nan's head. It was terrible to behold. Some sort of white spirit seemed to spring from Nan's head.

Tarak fell back. "No," he cried. "Spare me, O Spirit."

Nan paused in midstrike. Had he gone mad? Then she watched in horror as he grabbed a small child and held a sharp stick to its head.

"Go back to whence you came or I will sacrifice this child," he chattered.

It was at that moment that something inside Chandra seemed to shift and change. She became furious. She saw red. She felt hot with indignation. Her soul burned for justice.

To Tarak's great shock, the creature shifted its appearance. It became red and it seemed to grow. Its mouth opened and a long tongue of flame shot out toward him.

"Release that child," Chandra shouted. "Release him and be gone, you beast!"

Tarak's eyes went wide and unfocused in absolute terror. "Dragon," he wailed. "A tree dragon! Save me!"

"I said *be gone*," Chandra cried, and shot out her long tongue at him again.

By now Miss Nan had recovered her wits enough to realize who the "dragon" was. It was all she could do not to cry with relief or laugh with joy.

Her frightened little friend, always so careful not to make a wrong move, was saving their lives with her righteous rage.

Tarak dropped his weapon and fled the tree. He was never heard from again.

To this day, mothers tell their children of Chandra the Great Tree Dragon. They tell of the day when one tiny creature changed herself and the world around her, all for the better.

The Magpie

I n a meadow lived a magpie. From his perch the bird could see every creature that moved beneath. The magpie collected bits of things that it kept tucked away in its nest.

The magpie believed that the meadow belonged to him and everyone and everything that crossed beneath his tree was truly beneath him.

All the creatures in the meadow knew the magpie. They were very careful to say only things the bird liked to hear, and they did whatever he told them to do. This was because the magpie had a terrible temper and would often pelt those he did not like with hard, sharp things he had stored in his nest.

All the animals knew better than to cross the magpie.

It came to pass that a small field mouse took up residence in the hollow of the tree's roots. The mouse said a cheerful "good morning" to the bird every day. Each day the mouse offered to share some of the things he had collected with the bird.

Magpie was so furious at the appearance of this cheerful little intruder that at first he didn't even speak to the mouse. Then he recovered himself and began pelting the mouse with bits of things in an effort to get him to leave.

On the first day the bird dropped twigs and branches down on the mouse. Mouse very happily gathered the twigs and took them inside his burrow.

On the second day, the bird threw acorns and hard nuts down on the mouse, often leaving him red with welts and bruises.

Mouse collected the things and took them inside.

On the third day, the magpie was really seething with hatred for this mouse. How dare he invade Magpie's territory and then ignore the bird's best efforts to drive him away? The bird waited for the mouse to leave his hole and then rained a collection of stones down on him.

After licking his wounds, Mouse hauled the stones into his burrow.

On the fourth day, Mouse was out in the field and spotted a boy standing by the tree. The boy was laughing and standing over the magpie. He had felled the bird with his slingshot and was preparing to crush it beneath his boot.

Quick as a flash Mouse ran to the boy and bit him hard on the ankle. The boy shrieked and dropped his weapon. Then he ran home crying.

Mouse scurried over to Magpie and began to smooth his ruffled feathers. Then he went inside and brought out bits of cloth and some of the sticks the bird had used to pelt him and fashioned a stretcher.

He placed Magpie on the stretcher and pulled him into his burrow, where he nursed him back to health by feeding him acorn broth by a twig fire. He served the broth in stone bowl.

It took nearly a week before Magpie was well enough to speak. He could not believe that it was Mouse who had saved him.

When he could talk, the bird said, "Why? After the way I treated you, why would you save me?"

Mouse looked truly shocked by the bird's words.

"Why? After all the kindness you have shown me, how could I do otherwise?" Mouse said.

"Kindness!" gasped the magpie. He did not say more, because he was suddenly ashamed of what his real intentions had been.

"You gave me twigs for my fire and branches to build my furniture," Mouse said. "You gave me enough acorns and nuts to feed me through the winter and enough stones to make these fine bowls. True, your aim was often poor, but how could I be angry with so generous a neighbor?"

From that day on the magpie became truly generous, to Mouse and all the other animals in the meadow. He flew far and wide collecting bits to share with them.

Only now he was sure to give his offerings gently, and he never again cast a stone at a neighbor.

The Grackle

The rabbit was an angry fellow.

It seemed that nearly everything made him hopping mad.

In the morning when he woke, Rabbit was angry about having to get out of bed.

"I hate our house," he said grumpily. "Everything is old. I hate my toys because they're old and boring."

He looked at his stuffed animals, cars, books, and games and got even angrier. He threw them all on the floor and kicked them around. "Other rabbits have nicer things than I do," he said.

Then he was angry about having to eat carrots for breakfast. So he would not eat.

"Carrots are boring," he said, and twitched his whiskers and wrinkled his nose. "Other rabbits have much better food to eat than I do."

At lunchtime he was angry because, having skipped breakfast, he was very, very hungry.

When his mother offered to take him outside, he cried and shouted, "I hate being outside!"

When she told him he could stay in the house, he cried, "I hate being inside!"

So Rabbit spent most of his time sitting on the front porch.

One day, as Rabbit sat alone on his porch, he began to sniff the air. It smelled different. It smelled smoky.

Before he knew what was happening, his mother came hopping out of the house.

"Run! Run! The house is on fire," she shouted. "Run and get help."

For once, Rabbit did not argue. Rabbit ran.

Every house he came to was empty because it was market day. The only house where someone was home was the home of the grackle.

Nobody ever saw much of the grackle because he didn't like to have visitors and he seldom went to market. He was dirty, green, hairy, and he smelled awful.

Little rabbit raced up the path and saw the grackle sitting on his front porch.

"Help! Help! Our house is on fire and you are the only one who can help us," he cried.

The grackle looked angry.

"I hate house fires," snapped the grackle. "I hate people who need help putting them out. Go away!"

Rabbit could not believe what his long ears were hearing. This must surely be the meanest, most selfish animal that ever lived.

"But we need help," cried the rabbit again. "If you don't help us we will lose everything! We will lose our house and everything in it!"

Grackle laughed. "I have been watching you and listening to you. I see that you are just like me," he said. "You don't like anything except complaining and being alone."

With that the grackle pulled a mirror out of his pocket and held it up in front of the bunny. When Rabbit looked in the mirror he didn't see a bunny looking back. He saw instead a dirty, hairy, green, stinky creature in his bunny clothes.

Rabbit was too surprised to speak.

"What's so great about that old house of yours," the grackle asked. "All your toys are old. All your books are boring, and all you ever cook in that kitchen of yours is carrot soup. You should be happy to get rid of it all. Good riddance!"

"That's not true," the young rabbit said. "I have stuffed animals to cuddle at night, projects to build, and books about strange and wonderful places, and . . . and . . ."

Suddenly, the rabbit knew that he had been wrong to be so angry all the time.

The grackle held up the mirror again and this time the rabbit didn't see a grackle. Instead he saw a happy little bunny sitting at the table and eating carrot soup with his mother.

"Time to decide," said the grackle. "What do you want to be? A bunny or me?"

Rabbit knew. He said good-by.

He hopped home as fast as he could and when he got there he found that some neighbors coming home from the market had seen the smoke and put out the fire.

The house was saved, but everything inside was all smoky and covered with soot and many things were wet from the water used to put out the fire.

His mother looked very sad. "I am sorry," she said. "Everything is a big mess and dinner is burned."

To his mother's surprise, Rabbit smiled. He ran over and hugged her.

"I saw the grackle! He said our house was old and awful, and he was wrong," he cried. "He said I was being just like him, and he was right. I never want to be a grackle again."

His mother hugged him and smiled. "I have just the thing for you," she said.

From the closet she pulled a long flat box. She opened it up and took out a large mirror and hung it on the wall.

"When I was a little girl, I saw the grackle and he gave me this," she said. "Whenever I was feeling angry, I would run over and look in the mirror. If I saw a face that was looking grackly, I would make funny faces back until I started to laugh. Grackles never laugh. Then I never looked like the grackle again."

From that day on, whenever the little rabbit felt angry, he would run to the mirror and laugh his grackles away.

Birds in the Hand

The sandpipers liked to live a hectic life. On the edge of disaster the little flock of birds was always rushing to and fro. Thin legs sped from the dry sand to the foamy shore break and back again thousands of times a day. Needlelike beaks poked down into the wet sand to pluck out tidbits of food. Then all would speed away before the next wave could douse them.

Piper was not afraid of the waves because, like the others in his flock, all his life had been spent in concert with the tide, wind, and sand. He knew them as well as the beat of his own heart. What to others appeared to be fear was in fact the exhilaration of being a tiny creature that was one with powerful elements.

Unfortunately, the casual or careless observer only perceived a silly little bird in what appeared to be a futile and repetitive struggle for survival.

Such was the case of the gray and white seagulls wheeling overhead. They laughed out loud at the little birds' antics.

"Run, run, little ones," they would jeer. "Hurry, scurry, before the big wave gets you."

The gulls never rushed. Instead, they preferred to have their food tossed to them by the tourists and fishermen who frequented the area.

Of course this competition for what little was there often led to a feeding frenzy, especially when a large group of gulls came in to feed. They would peck and scratch each other while fighting for the scraps tossed their way.

"This is the proper way to live," said Skree, the leader of the gull pack. "No rushing about, just see what you want and go after it. You fight for what you want and then you sit back and enjoy it all. Only the strong survive."

Skree was proud of his battle scars. His left wing was tattered but functional, his feathers stained with the blood of his rivals. He was stout and prosperous. Skree and the others were comfortable with their way of life, which also included occasionally stealing choice bits such as ice cream cones from small unwary children who walked the beach.

Skree had earned his position as leader of the pack. He sent his scouts out to look for potential food sources. They were trained to call when they had found their mark. Then Skree and the rest would swoop in and the frenzy would begin.

Piper and his flock were only peripherally aware of the practices of the gulls. They could hear them coming and going and were always sure to get out of the way when the gulls were about to descend. For the most part, the little flock did not make it their business to deal with the gulls.

"It is a wise bird that knows its limitations. We are small and fast but all of us put together could not fight off the gulls in a moment of frenzy," said the eldest sandpiper. He was known as Dryfoot, for he was said to be so quick and agile that he never dampened his feet on the race from shore to dune.

One morning, as Piper was gathering breakfast from the shimmering, foam-washed sand, he heard a keening sound. He rushed several steps so as to be clear of the next wave and then looked up.

A little girl was making the terrible sound. Her heels were dug into the wet sand and her short, damp fingers clung desperately to the leg of an old rag doll. The long hair of the doll was in Skree's viselike grip.

An awful tug-of-war was taking place. The child's guardian was nowhere in sight, and a nasty pack of fat gulls was beating its wings all around her.

"Mine, mine," the child wailed. "You bad, bad, bird! Let go!"

Skree had taken the doll's flowing hair for a tasty treat when he first saw it and, bold from years of being unchallenged, he had dived on the child and tried to wrench it away.

Once he realized his error, he was going to let go, but his minions had gathered around and he did not wish to show that he was mistaken.

Only the strong survive, and those who were seen as lacking judgment were also regarded as being weak in body. It was not long before the pack would turn on such a bird and kill it.

To Skree this doll represented his power to rule. He must have it. He must show them all that he was still fit and strong. He squeezed his eyes tight shut so as not to see the child's tears. He tugged and tugged at the doll and tried to pull the child off balance. He must have the doll at any cost.

With his eyes shut and the deafening sound of the cheers of his pack, Skree could not tell which way he was moving.

Piper was so horrified by what he saw that he stood stock-still for the first time in his entire life. He stood and stared. He was frozen by the image before him. He saw the little girl and the bird, both blind with need. Both were locked in combat over a bit of rag and yarn. Both were headed into the churning surf.

"Piper," cried Dryfoot. "Look away. Look away this instant. There is nothing you can or should do here. You are of no use in such large affairs. You have a family to look after."

Try as he might, Piper could not turn away.

"At least move away before the waves get you as well," Dryfoot shouted. "Move! Move now!"

Move he did, but it was not away from the water and the struggle. He raced at a speed never before seen by any sandpiper. Like a tiny bolt of lightning, he streaked into the fray.

Knowing that he could not fly high or hard enough to attack the gull, he headed instead for the child. He raced to her and drove his pointy beak into her little foot. With a shriek of surprise the child let go of the doll and reached down to rub the wound.

Letting go of the doll meant that all the force Skree had been exerting came back at him. He fell backward with the doll still in his beak, tumbling helplessly into the face of a massive wave just as it was about to break on shore. He was swept under and pounded into the gritty shell-strewn bottom.

As he went under and rolled, he thought frantically, "I can still save myself. I must keep hold of this thing so that when I rise from the water, I will have my prize to show them all. They will see my strength and I will rule them forever."

Meanwhile, her thrashing about in fear and frustration resulted in the child's kicking Piper with all her might. The kick sent him sprawling in the wet sand, where he lay for a long painful while.

He lay very still and thought about what he had done.

"Stupid me," he thought bitterly. "I should have listened to Dryfoot. I will surely die here for my efforts. 'Never a good deed goes unpunished,' is what he always says. He was right again."

Piper heard a groan and opened his eyes to see where it came from. It was Skree, now lying broken and dying beside him. The doll had swelled in the sea and filled his beak, propping it open and allowing his belly and lungs to fill with salt water.

The gulls and sandpipers all gathered around their fallen comrades, forming one large circle.

"Stupid little bird," growled a large gull. "If he hadn't interfered, our leader would not be dying. I will finish him off with a stomp of my webbed foot."

Dryfoot intervened. "Your leader is dying by his own pride," he said. "His need to prove his strength was his weakness. Piper's compassion for both your leader and the child has proven him to be the best of us all."

It was just then that the voice of the child was heard, and the birds backed away as she and her guardian approached.

The guardian was a very tall man with kind eyes that seemed to shift color with his mood. Looking at the child, they were dazzling blue. When his gaze fell on the two flocks of birds, they shifted to a flinty gray. When he turned to the two fallen birds, they went to a sorrowful hazel-green.

He carried the child in his arms and set her down near the two wounded birds.

"See now, Little One, that these two birds are living creatures, and the doll is only a toy that has no heart or soul," he said softly. "While the gull was cruel and meant to steal the doll from you, it was still a living thing, and its life was worth more than the toy."

The big man reached down and eased the swollen doll from Skree's beak. He stroked down the rumpled feathers and then carefully lifted Skree and held him in his palm. He took a white handkerchief and wrapped Skree in it and put him gently in the oversized pocket of his large white jacket.

"I can heal him," he said. "I will take him home with me and he will not die. Though he was a sad creature, I can rehabilitate him."

"Now this brave little soul," he said as he carefully lifted Piper and wrapped him in another white cloth. "He's a bad bird, too," the child interrupted. "He hurt me."

The big man chuckled. "Judge not too quickly, child," he said. "Though he caused you pain in forcing you to let go of the doll, his action spared your life. You needed someone to force your hand in order to save you. You were close to drowning and could not see the danger."

He gently stroked Piper's tiny brow. "He has wisdom that needs to be nurtured, that he might heal and teach others. I will take him with me as well.

The child looked up at the big man and smiled. He always made such good sense and always, made her feel so much better.

"Now I must go home with these two," he said. "You sit here and wait for your mother."

With that the big man winked his eye, and then blinked away like a reflection of the sun on the water.

All the birds were humbled by what they had seen and heard. Slowly they arose headed off to their own places to ponder it all.

"Margeaux! Margeaux," cried the child's mother as she rushed up the beach. "Where have you been? I have looked everywhere for you."

"I was right here with my guardian" she said. "Well, he has gone now, but he was right here. He had to go fix some birds."

The mother shook her head. Margeaux and her imaginary friend again, she thought. It was a charming story her daughter told everyone, all about how, upon being born, she had met a guide on her way down from heaven and had kept him as a friend.

The mother asked, "When will you stop seeing your invisible guardian, my child? You are getting to be a big girl. Soon you must have real friends instead of this spirit."

Little Margeaux's eyes looked deeply into those of her mother. The child took on a queer expression, as if she were listening to a voice that no one else could hear.

Then she answered, "I think it would be better if you meet him first, Mama. Once you get to know him, you won't want him to go away either."

Fern Finds Home

eep in the house of the forest where it was dark and cool, the moss carpeted the floor, toadstools bordered the rooms, and vines wove a tapestry on the walls.

In the center of the great hall grew a delicate green plant whose many, leaf-covered arms reached out to those around her.

Into this peaceful place came a snake.

"So pure and beautiful," it said. "I have never seen anything so radiant."

Around and around the plant the snake began to circle.

"Hello, my dear," it said. "It is a lovely home you have here. You must be very proud. Yes, you must. You must."

Fern trembled, for the snake had a way of talking and moving that was so smooth as to be almost hypnotic.

Even though the house of the forest did not belong to her, she answered, "Oh, thank you. It is very nice. Yes, I should be proud."

Fern wondered why she had given such an answer. She could no more take credit for the beautiful dwelling than could the snake. Yet somehow he made her feel as if no other force existed but his words.

She swayed, and had to shake herself to focus her attention.

"I am sorry," she recovered. "The house of the forest is not mine. I am only a small part of the home that the creator made."

The snake circled closer and embraced the plant in his coils.

"Why, that is ridiculous," he hissed slyly. "You are the center of the house. It is you who make it special. You have grown here all on your own. You alone have spread your arms and provided beauty in this dark, dank place."

Fern thought for a moment. She was confused and shaken. The house had never seemed dark or dank before.

Yet the snake seemed to make sense. He made her feel proud and strong to think that she alone had grown and thrived.

She had never before felt strong, only delicate, and often weak.

She had always relied on her faith that the creator of all things was in charge of the house of the forest and that she was merely a part of the design.

Suddenly it seemed much better to be a powerful being than a simple one, growing quietly in the midst of others.

"Why, yes," she said giddily. "You are right of course. I have been so silly. The power is in me, not some force I have never seen or heard."

The snake's coils began to tighten, and she could feel herself being torn from her roots.

Snake had his plan. He thought the plant so beautiful that if he swallowed her, then he too would radiate as she did.

"What is happening?" she cried in terror. "What are you doing?"

The snake began to swallow her whole. Before long she was in his belly, dissolving with every moment that passed.

She could hear him laughing. "Now I shall have all that beauty for myself," he said.

To the house of the forest he shouted, "You lose again."

Fern's last thought was, "The power was in me, but it was not my own."

Then there was darkness.

Fern opened her eyes to see the house of the forest around her once again. The snake was gone.

A light was streaming down upon her from the canopy of leaves above. She had grown back from her roots in the forest floor.

"Thank you," she said softly. "I know where I come from now. I will not forget again."

From that day forward Fern spread her arms and became more radiant than ever before.

A Dog's Life

Once there lived a dog that had a happy life. The dog's name was Mot.

Mot lived in a big house with all the food he could eat, and he slept in a warm bed by the fireplace.

Every day the old man who owned the house would come to sit with the dog and stroke his head and tell Mot of the places he had visited during the day.

The man was a storyteller and made his living by traveling from village to village and making up special stories for the children. In return, the people gave him gold coins.

The man used the coins to buy food and pay for his house. All of the best bits of food he bought went to his faithful, furry friend.

To the man his dog was not a pet, but a loyal and trusted friend.

He looked forward to his time at the end of the day when he could share his food and his stories with his furry friend.

One day, while the man was away, Mot sat outside.

Up walked a dog he had never seen before. She was the most beautiful creature he had ever seen.

While Mot was dark and scruffy, she was light and shiny.

Her name was Mimmy and Mot fell instantly in love with her.

When the man came home from his day's travels, he saw Mimmy and smiled. He made a bed by the fireplace for her and she and Mot curled up happily together.

They lived happily for some time until one day Mot noticed that Mimmy was looking very angry.

Whenever the man passed by her, she let out a low grrrrrrrrrrah sound.

When the man left for the day, Mot asked her what was wrong.

"I don't like him," she growled. "He has so much, but he only throws us the scraps from his table. He makes us sleep on the floor. If he really loved us he would build big beds for us and feed us at his table."

Mot did not know what to say. He had never thought of this before. He had always felt more like the man's son than his pet. Now, listening to Mimmy, he suddenly saw things differently.

That night when the man came home and reached out to stroke Mot's fur, Mot pulled away and growled.

When he placed the food in front of Mot, the dog knocked over the bowl and jumped up to the table and ate the man's supper instead.

The man was shocked.

Then Mimmy joined in and the two dogs growled and snarled at the old man.

When the man tried to calm the dogs he was knocked down so hard that he lay there for a very long time.

When he finally got up, there were tears in his eyes.

He opened the door and, using a broom, shooed the dogs out of his house.

The old man sat and stared into the fire, wondering what could have so upset the animals.

For now he saw them as animals and not his friends.

"Well," said Mimmy, with pride. "That should teach the man! He will never treat us so poorly again. Now he will get lonely and when we come back to scratch at his door, he will take us in and treat us better."

Mot was not so sure about Mimmy's ideas anymore. He began to feel very sad and empty inside.

After a few days passed he looked in the window of the old man's house and saw that the man lay in his bed looking very sick.

Mot remembered all the times the man had stroked his fur and fed him and told him stories.

Mimmy came up to Mot and said, "It is not time to scratch at the door!"

Mot turned around and said grrrrrrrrrrrrrrrah! at her.

"Look what we have done," he cried. "The old man is sick at heart and cannot go out to tell his stories. He will starve!"

"Who cares about him?" Mimmy said. "He did not love you. I love you and now all you should care for is me."

With those words Mot realized that Mimmy had been greedy. Also, she was jealous of his friendship with the old man.

"Mimmy," said Mot. "You are my new friend and I love you, but that does not mean I cannot love my old friends as well. The old man has truly been good to me and I must go to him."

Mimmy was angry and said she would leave and never come back.

This made Mot sad, but he knew how much the old man needed him.

"Come or go as you like," Mot said. "I will always be here to love you and feed you, just as the old man has been here for me. But I must be true to my old friend."

Mimmy went to the window and looked in.

She saw the old man lying beneath the covers and looking very sad.

Suddenly she knew she had been terribly wrong. She had never had a friend like him. She realized she had been jealous of the kind way he treated Mot.

"You go to him and I will gather some wood for the fire," she said. "He must be very cold."

Mot ran to the door of the house and barked and scratched and jumped until the old man finally got out of bed to answer his calls.

When he saw Mot, the old man was afraid that the dog might attack him again. Then Mot came and stood very close to the man and stood very still.

The man smiled and stroked the dog's fur.

When the man sat by the fireplace, the dog brought him a blanket and curled up beside him.

When Mimmy scratched at the door, the old man let her

in. She placed the sticks by the fire.

Then, feeling badly about how she had behaved, she turned to leave.

The old man called her back. He stroked her fur and said kind words to her.

Then he went to a cupboard and pulled out two beautiful wooden bowls. One said Mot and the other, Mimmy.

He placed them at a special dog-sized table beside his own and invited the dogs to dine.

They all ate and were happy ever after, while the old man told his stories.

IN THE
MIDDLE

Cat's Cradle

Catania the tabby had three kittens. The first, a boy, was a gray-and-black tiger stripe with green eyes. The second, also a boy, was gray with white paws and black eyes. The last was white as a ball of snow with glittering gray eyes—a little girl.

It wasn't long before the three little kittens were romping and playing with each other. All three were smart and fast. They made their mother very proud indeed.

As time went by, however, the mother began to notice that the little white kitten had grown quiet and drawn away from the others. Worried that it might be ill, Catania took the kitten to the Doctor Tom.

He poked and prodded and found that the kitten was well and healthy after all. "Just a phase," he reassured Catania. "Mothers worry too much about their kittens."

But the little white kitten spent more and more time away from others. The kitten kept to herself in her corner of the basket. More often than she liked to admit, Catania found her little one curled beneath the covers in fear of the world.

At first she was sympathetic, but by the time the kitten became a young cat, Catania was at her wit's end.

"Get out and see the world," she yowled. "There's nothing to be afraid of."

It was not to be. The young cat dug her claws into the mattress and refused to be drawn away.

Because the white cat took up so much of Catania's time, her two sons had grown resentful of the kitten and teased it unmercifully.

"Scairdy cat, fraidy cat. Afraid of this. Afraid of that," they chanted at her. They could not understand how a full-grown cat could lie about all day in bed and only come out for meals and trips to the litter box.

To White Heart, for that was the cat's name, it was not laziness that kept her in bed. She wanted more than anything to go out and see the world, but it all seemed so huge and overwhelming.

On sunny days all she could see were the long dangerous shadows cast by everything around her. On cloudy days she hid from the sound of the rain tapping angrily on the roof and battering at the windows.

When her brothers were adopted and went to new homes to start their lives as house cats, she was left behind. She had hidden under the bed and lashed out when the giant hands had tried to snatch her. The poor creature had stayed flattened against the wall beneath the bed for days before her mother was finally able to coax her out.

So it was that White Heart stayed with her mother. The only thing that she would do with her time was to weave yarn into her own creations. They were beautiful and fanciful, spun like cobwebs in varying shades. Some were somber in blue and gray. Others were bold in red and yellow. All were miraculous. All were tucked away beneath the basket because White Heart was too frightened to show them for fear of what others might say.

Years passed, and Catania grew old and sad. Her boys never visited because they did not wish to see their sister. She frightened them. They were afraid that there, but for the grace of nature, went their lives. When they looked at White Heart they were afraid that someday they might change and become like her.

Finally, as her time to die drew near, Catania called her sons to come and be with her. "When I am gone, one of you must take your sister in," she said.

The air was immediately thickened by their caterwauling. "Ma," said Tig, the striped cat. "I have little ones at home. I cannot take in a mad cat! Be reasonable. Leave her to Char to care for."

"Oh no," cried Char, the gray. "Not I. Last time I tried to talk sense to her she bit me. No, she must fend for herself or go to a shelter."

Not a shelter. They were the worst places on Earth. Catania was in despair at the thought of her baby ending up in a place like that. After her boys had gone, she decided to go to old Dr. Tom and ask his advice.

The old cat paced and considered. Then he brought out a bag of leaves and placed them carefully in a large pillow case.

"This may seem odd," he said. "But some of these cats have been found to come around after sleeping on catnip pillows. It lightens their moods and helps them go out into the world."

Desperate for any relief, Catania took the pillow home and gave it to White Heart. At first she was suspicious of the new thing in her basket, but by and by she came to sleep on it.

Days went by and weeks and months with little change. Then one morning Catania awoke to an amazing sight. She saw her daughter up and about and obviously preparing for an outing.

"I thought I'd go out for a short explore," White Heart said hesitantly. "Is it allowed?"

Weak with joy, Catania nodded her approval.

As the weeks went by, Tig and Char began to visit regularly. White Heart began to speak freely to the family of her fears and even spoke of plans for the future.

For the first time, she showed her weaving to her mother and brothers and was pleased to see their approval.

"These are the most beautiful things I have ever seen," Catania told her daughter. "You have a gift. What do you call them?"

A bit uneasy with the attention, White Heart hesitated. Then she said, "I call them Feeling Shawls. I weave them to match the moods I see around me."

She pulled out a beautiful pink and white froth of a shawl and gave it to her mother. "This one is you. It is love and faith."

Then she took out one of dark umber and gray and gave it to Tig. "This is yours. It is brooding and fear."

The next was a striking combination of reds and rusty colors. "This one is yours Char. It is anger and resentment."

Her brothers shuffled their paws. In shame, each tucked his shawl under his arm.

"Which is yours, daughter?" Catania asked.

White Heart took out a thick woolen shawl. The topside was jet black with threads of deep blue running through it. It was dark and impenetrable as a moonless night. Then she turned it to the underside. What was underneath was a wild dance of colors. Reds warred with yellows and spread into white and amber—a sunburst.

The truth of what they were seeing made her brothers weep. They recovered themselves and took turns gathering her into their paws for an embrace.

"Will you turn your shawl and wear it inside out now?" asked Tig.

"No," said White Heart. "I will weave a new one with hues on both sides. I will weave new shawls for both you and Char as well. Now that we have all shown our true colors."

Rabbit's Humbling Experience

oney is often a good thing to have. It is not necessary to have great piles of it cluttering up the place and attracting thieves, mind you, but a bit of it here and there can be a very comforting thing indeed. Rabbit knew this well because he didn't have any.

Not that Rabbit wasn't a hard worker. He worked long hours to support himself, his wife, and four little bunnies.

No, the problem was that money just didn't go as far as it used to, and having a burrowful of little ones to care for seemed to make it vanish faster than ever.

Little Pansy needed braces for her teeth. Kip needed a winter coat and all of them could do with new shoes at least once a year. Life peppered the little brood with challenges like leaky pipes that cost an ear and a whisker to repair. Last year the carrot crop failed completely due to drought.

While they weren't as poor as church mice; they were barely keeping body and soul together.

The problem was not just the lack of money, but the lack of faith Rabbit had in others and in himself.

Whenever there was a problem with finances, Rabbit would try to solve it all himself. He tried to make sure that Mrs. Rabbit never saw how much strain he was under or how poor they really were.

"She is my love, my all," he fretted to himself. "She must never know how I have failed her and the children."

It was the same in all that he undertook. At work he refused to give more than tiny problems to his underlings to solve. So he was constantly buried in work. Projects from his department were always finished just under the wire because he was the one doing most of the work.

After a while his coworkers began to feel that he did not trust them to do a good job. Many of them left and went to other companies.

"Just a pack of unreliables," he told his boss when asked why he was running late again. "If you want something done right, do it yourself."

The truth of the matter was that Mr. Rabbit was afraid of letting go of so much as a crumb of responsibility for fear that people would think he was not a hard worker. Worse! What if another rabbit could do a better job than he did? He would be out of a job.

It was true that he could have asked his younger brother for help, but he would never allow himself to be diminished in his brother's eyes. He was the eldest of seven and should be the most successful of them all. Besides, his brother would likely demand every detail of how he had failed and he could not bear to tell.

All this, Rabbit carried inside him like a stone weighing down on his heart. Today was the day when the stone would nearly crush him.

He had come home as usual, but tonight the burrow was dark as pitch. Fearing the worst, he hurried inside to find his family eating by candlelight.

"What's all this?" he asked his wife.

Mrs. Rabbit was a very nervous bunny at this moment for she had to tell her husband that their electric service had been cut off. She knew it was her fault for not paying the charge on time, but some months back she had discovered that their bank account was nearly empty.

Being afraid that her husband might think she had spent too much money on the things the family needed, she chose not to speak to him about the problem. Instead she took in washing and baked bread and made jams to sell at the farm market.

Mrs. Rabbit had hidden the bills and paid them when she could. She scrimped and saved and did more odd jobs. She refused to ask anyone for help. That would be too humiliating.

"How on Earth could you have let these bills go for so long without payment?" Mr. Rabbit demanded as he pounded his fist on the table.

Mrs. Rabbit went cold with dread. "We just didn't have the money," she said. There, it was out now. "We needed the water and the carrot seeds. I made some jams and bread to sell. I thought I would sell enough jam this month to pay for it, but that big storm forced them to close the farm market for over a week."

Mr. Rabbit paced and fretted. He was embarrassed that his wife had known of their finances and had never said a word. He was angry that she had taken it upon herself to earn the money. He became angry at her deception.

His anger passed into a deep feeling of depression and failure. For the first time in his life he had to admit defeat.

"I am so sorry, my love," he said as a large tear rolled down his furry cheek. "I have failed you miserably. I suppose you will leave me now. I wouldn't blame you."

Mrs. Rabbit had been prepared for the worst. She had been ready for him to rant and rave or walk out and leave her for being so incompetent. Never had she imagined that she would hear these words. She had never seen her husband cry. She was frozen in place.

Misunderstanding her lack of response, Mr. Rabbit rose and slowly began to gather his things to leave. "Better to go than to be tossed out," he thought. She would surely find a better rabbit to provide for her and the children.

Realizing what her husband was about to do snapped Mrs. Rabbit into action. "I'm sorry," she cried. "Oh, so sorry for disappointing you. Please don't leave me. I love you with all my heart."

Love him? He had failed. How could she still love him?

"But I failed you," he managed. "I should go and let you start again with a more worthy partner."

Mrs. Rabbit went to him and put her arms around him as if he were one of her small bunnies. She stroked his head and murmured soothing words.

Then she began to laugh. She laughed and laughed, until tears spilled down her cheeks.

"We're quite a pair aren't we?" she gasped out. "We were both so busy being unworthy and afraid that we didn't share the burden."

Mr. Rabbit was listening, but he was still not sure he saw her point. "That's all well and good, but it doesn't get the lights turned on or the water flowing into the pipes," he said.

Though it nearly killed him to say it aloud, he asked, "What are we going to do?"

Mrs. Rabbit drew a deep breath. "We are going to borrow the money."

"Never," he exploded. "Never in my life have I asked anyone for anything, and I'll not start now."

Eyeing him carefully, she made her choice. "No, you won't do the asking. I will," she said and held up a paw as if to ward off his response. "Humble is better than frightened in my book. I have been living in a state of terror for months now, and just the thought of getting help suddenly takes the weight of the world off me."

Mr. Rabbit looked at his wife. How had he failed to see how strong she was? How had he missed such an obvious solution?

He put his arms around his wife and looked into her eyes. "No. You will not ask," he said.

Before she could dispute him, he added, "We will go together. We will share the load. We will go to my brother and ask for a loan. Then I will tell my employer that I need a raise. If he will not give it, then I will take a second job."

He added, "There are going to be some changes around here. This family is no longer suffering in silence. We will share the worries as partners, and when they become too great for just us two, we will share them again with family or friends."

So their troubles passed. In time they made their way in the world. It was not the last time the little family would have to accept aid from friends or relatives, but it was the last time they would hate themselves for being in need.

When their fortunes increased, it did not come through fear and deceit, but by learning to be trusting and humble. They would never forget their hardships.

When at last the day came when they could help others, they gave freely and without question. They had learned that for many it is harder to receive than to give.

The Twisted Tree

In a garden, surrounded by tall pine trees fell a little, fuzzy green seedpod.

It was a beautiful bright green, pointed at both ends and was soft as velvet.

The pod landed on a clear patch of dirt between two trees. One was a brash young cedar, the other a thin pine.

As the days and weeks passed, the wind blew and stirred the dirt, which covered the pod. Rain fell on the pod and later the sun shone down and warmed it.

From the pod grew long, velvety, green shoots that stretched up into the air.

When the wind blew the strands twisted together and wound around each other like an emerald rope.

Years passed; the shoots grew up into thick brown branches and touched the two trees.

The body of the tree was twisted like a corkscrew, but the arms grew long and straight and reached out to hold on to the two trees on either side.

The Cedar and pine trees had never seen anything like the twisted tree. They began to argue about it.

Cedar was worried about the way it was clinging to them.

"It could choke us," it said. "It could overshadow us and make us wither and die."

Pine said, "Don't be so silly. The way it hugs me makes me feel loved. I like the way it supports us and binds us to each other."

"I don't need support," huffed Cedar. "We were just fine all this time. We don't need this twisted thing here."

The twisted tree could hear the other trees, but could not talk, as the others did.

It didn't want the other trees to be afraid of it, so it found other ways to show love for them.

In the spring the twisted one sprouted hundreds of tiny purple flowers. From top to bottom the twisted tree and the two trees on either side were covered in a blanket of purple.

Cedar cried out, "This is terrible! People will come to gather the flowers and cut us down by mistake!"

"Nonsense," said Pine. "People will come to sit under the purple flower trees and they will take special care of us because we bring them so much happiness."

As it happened, a man saw the flowering twisted tree and built a bench around the trunk where people could come and sit. Artists painted pictures of the trees. Children danced around them.

"What if the twisted tree falls," Cedar demanded. "It will drag us down."

Pine laughed until its leaves shook. "All your worrying will fell you before anything else has the chance," Pine said.

As it happened there was a terrible storm, and both Cedar and Pine were badly damaged by the wind.

The twisted tree was like a spring, able to bend and rock with the wind. It could see that its neighbors were in danger and held on with all its might to save them. Instead of falling it held the other two trees in place while they healed.

As time passed and the flowers faded away, the twisted tree sprouted hundreds of long, fuzzy, green velvety pods. The pods fell all around the garden. Birds, squirrels and even the wind carried many of the pods away to other gardens where they could grow. People who like the purple flowers gathered the pods to plant in their own gardens. Those that stayed behind began to sprout little twisted vines.

The twisted tree had given everything it had to the earth. It was very tired, but very proud of its gift.

"This is terrible," cried Cedar. "Twisted trees will take over the earth! We will be surrounded!"

Pine shook a branch at its old friend.

"You have not learned much over the years, have you my friend," Pine said. "Now all the trees in the garden and on the earth will have the love and support we have enjoyed over the years. Every spring the earth will be covered in fresh, purple flowers. It will all be beautiful."

And so it was.

Bird's Paradise

Two little birds were building their nests one day when they began to speak of what would make them happiest.

The birds, both of them sporting bright yellow feathers, had always been friends. For as long as either could remember they had shared their hopes and dreams.

"I wish to find contentment and perfect peace," said the first bird.

After a moment's thought the other bird agreed that this would be the best thing to attain.

The conflict between the old friends came when they began to discuss how to achieve their common goal.

The first bird said he would like to travel and meet animals of every type and size.

"I will fly far and wide to see all that there is to see and learn something new from everyone I meet," he said. "Someone I meet is sure to know how to have perfect peace and contentment."

His friend was shocked. "Nonsense," he chirped. "In order to achieve contentment you must have a good solid nest, plenty of food, a mate and a few chicks. That is what I will do."

Well the two bickered long into the night until they finally decided to set it as a contest. They would part company for a period of ten years. At the end of that time they would meet on this very spot to compare their progress.

Unfortunately, each was so intent on proving himself correct and so insulted by the other's lack of approval that they parted in anger.

The bird that flew far and wide met many different sorts of animals in his travels. He saw how different other places and animals could be. Then, as time passed, he began to see how much they could be the same. He learned that everyone needed food and shelter and love to be happy.

He was becoming so contented with his new life that time passed very quickly. He sang beautiful songs for his supper and slept under the stars. Although he never took a wife he had a great love for his fellow creatures and having so many friends, he always had a place to be warm and safe.

He did not have his old friend. He remembered all of the angry words he had spoken to his friend before leaving home, and so did not know peace.

While the first bird was off travelling, the second yellow bird worked hard to build a fine nest and attract a wonderful mate. Their chicks were many and they were all strong and happy.

The second bird became very close to the community he lived in and was a kind a generous soul with his neighbors.

He too found contentment. Not having his old and dear friend, he did not know peace.

Finally the ten years came to an end and the birds flew to the appointed meeting place. In a rush the two creatures chirped away, detailing their experiences.

When they had finally finished they stood and looked at each other for a long while.

"So you have indeed found contentment, just as you predicted," the first bird said.

The other said a hesitant "yes" and added, "You too have found your contentment."

Neither felt peace.

As they stood there wondering where they had failed a large golden bird flew down from the sky and landed between them.

"I am the Bird of Paradise," she said in a golden voice. "I have watched you both for many years. You are both so close to attaining your goal. To do it you must work together."

The Bird of Paradise told them that they must forgive each other their angry words, spoken so long ago.

"You must also do something much harder," she said. "You must forgive yourselves."

With that the divine bird vanished. The two old friends embraced and forgave.

They lived the rest of their lives as they had lived the past ten years only now both had found peace and contentment within themselves. For peace and contentment are not things to be proved, but to be lived and savored, each in his own way.

How do I know this tale for the telling, you ask? A little bird told me.

Cricket Changes Her Tune

ricket hopped nervously from place to place. Always fretting.

"So much to do," she chirped. "Everyone is listening to me. Every night and day, every note must be perfect."

Truth be told, cricket really did have a gift for reaching others with her music. She could change her tune to suit her listener.

If ant was sad, cricket could perk him up with a bouncy melody. When the walking stick was being a stick in the mud she could liven his step with a reel or jig. When all the insects were in a tizzy over a coming storm cricket calmed them with a hymn or ballad.

Unfortunately, that responsibility had begun to weigh cricket's heart. If she were readying for a concert or even dinner with friends her tone became shrill.

"What! What do you want," she would screech at her little ones when they disturbed her at her tasks. "Can't you see I am busy? Don't you know that everyone is depending on me?"

After a while cricket's atonal whinges began to carry on the wind to where those outside her home could hear her.

"What horrid noise is that," groaned the caterpillar,

as she lay stretched on a twig. " It sounds like a rusty hinge on a door that is being repeatedly slammed."

The other insects listened and agreed. Something was wrong with their reliable and once harmonious friend.

A small delegation decided to ask the one bug they knew had the most wisdom. They went to visit the praying mantis and told him of their friend's plight.

"Mmmm," he said, cocking his great green head to one side. "I shall see about this."

So it came to pass that praying mantis sent cricket an invitation to tea. Cricket was so nervous about this great occasion that she nearly worried herself and her family to death in the hours before the meeting.

"It must be perfect," she shrilled as she tore about the house primping and practicing. "He must be in great need to have called upon me. I can't let him down. Oh dear, dear!"

Finally, much to everyone's relief, she rushed off to tea.

Upon arriving cricket immediately set about trying to sense mantis's mood. Was he sad? Had he been injured? What did he need that her music could heal?

To her dismay, she found the great mantis to be utterly unreadable. She felt he had no need at all. He appeared completely at peace. Finally, she suffered the humiliation of having to ask what it was he needed of her.

Slowly blinking his enormous eyes the mantis said, "You have been given a very great gift . . ."

Cricket hastily interrupted, "Thank you. You are too kind. I am only here to serve."

"Yes you are," mantis said solemnly. "Unfortunately you have been rather a poor tool of late."

Cricket was so horrified and overwhelmed that she began to cry. Great racking sobs and chirps filled the air.

"But I tried so hard," she said miserably. "I have worked until exhaustion trying to do well."

"That is just the problem," mantis said. "You are trying too hard."

Mantis told cricket to sit down and close her eyes. "Now," he said. "Think back to when you first began to play your tunes for others. What were you thinking of then?"

Cricket realized that she hadn't been thinking of anything. She had simply seen someone and felt happy or sad or compassionate, and her music had simply come from her soul to fill the air and heal the others around her.

"Now," he added, "Think back to what happened to make you leap off on your own."

Cricket pondered. "I lost faith in myself," she said. "I stopped trusting what guided me and began to fear."

Fear turned to panic and panic to anger and anger turned to fear again.

"Now go back to your family and friends," said mantis. "Take your faith back with you, and you will soon change your tune."

What's Good for the Goose

A t winter's end, the geese flew north. They settled into the area around a pretty little lake and set about making the place home.

Once they were settled, the female geese began to lay eggs in the nests they had carefully prepared.

Every year it was the same, thought May. Every year the other geese would lay their eggs and be rewarded with a string of fuzzy goslings to follow them about. Every year May lost a little more hope as her nest remained empty.

She had so much love to give. She pictured being the best mother. She would read them stories and wipe their tears. She would rock them and sing to them and teach them to fly long distances. Her heart ached from the love and longing inside.

"It just isn't meant to be," her partner honked. "Some geese just aren't born to be parents. Why don't you go over and see if you could help some of the others with their chicks? That would make you feel better."

This suggestion, as always, made May's emotions churn. It made her angry and jealous to think of being with someone else's goslings. It made her hurt deep inside and broke her heart a little with each passing season.

May found ways to pull herself away from the hurt. She did it by pulling away from her fellow geese. When the young mothers and their small charges waddled past she would make tisking noises and turn up her bill.

"Humph," she snorted when a particularly noisy brood went past. "A mother ought to be able to keep her children in line. Such behavior is unseemly!"

"Honk," she exclaimed, when a group of older goslings found a mud puddle to play in and became drippy messes. Then she gabbled, "Where is their mother? Who is in charge here? What a filthy mess. I am so glad I never chose to have any little ruffians."

Her partner watched in sorrow as his mate became old before her time. Her feathers turned white and her shortsightedness required that she wear little wiry spectacles.

She found fault with everything and everyone. "You spend too much of your time just floating about on the lake and daydreaming," she sniped at her spouse.

In her mind May blamed him for their lack of children. She thought that if he had wanted them as badly as she then they would have had packs of them by this time. This was a better alternative to admitting what was in her heart —she believed that she had failed.

May hated herself. She was so deeply angry with herself that she could not contain it. Her contempt for her body's failure spewed out onto everyone around her.

Yet, even as she chided and criticized she wished she could stop the words. But the dam in her soul had burst one day, and there was no repairing it now.

After a while it seemed to May as if she were no longer herself and so had no responsibility for her behavior. The real May seemed to be trapped in a floating bubble that hovered above her. From the bubble she could see clearly her missteps and bad deeds, but was powerless to stop herself.

She had removed herself from life and left behind an empty shell. The shell had cracked and the sharp fragments pricked at anyone who came near her.

The young mothers all steered clear of May and her sharp eye for faults. Her partner flew away. May was alone.

She told herself that this was a good thing. Having others around was a nuisance. The bubble that contained her true nature began to float higher and farther away until it seemed it would wink out of existence.

One evening, after a particularly annoying day, May sat by the lake. It was getting on to Fall and she knew she must soon migrate south with the others, but she was tired. So tired that she fell asleep and dreamed.

In her dream she saw herself as a gosling. She was in a meadow filled with wildflowers. The sun was shining, and she was chasing after butterflies. One beautiful white butterfly caught her eye and she followed it across the meadow and to the edge of a dark forest.

The butterfly flitted high in the sky, and if she had chosen to spread her wings, she could have followed. Instead she was drawn to the wood. She thought the cool darkness appealing.

Owls hooted and made her jump. Gnarled trees seemed to be reaching down to grab her, and every step she took was on boggy and acrid smelling ground. The butterfly was gone. She called out to it and was surprised to hear herself calling her own name.

"May! May! Where are you," she cried into the dark wood.

To her relief she heard her own voice calling to her from the other side of a big pile of bracken. She followed the voice until she came through the woods and into a clearing.

She shrieked when she saw the horrible looking old crone before her. The old goose was white with age, bent with loathing and blind with self-pity.

"So you finally found me," it said. "Like what you see?"

The young May shook with fear. "What do you want," she asked.

"I want to be you again," the old crone said. "I want to be young and full of hope. I want to chase butterflies and read stories to goslings. I want to be loved again."

In her dream, May looked at the old crone and felt pity for her and love. She went to her and the two geese, young and old, held each other for a long while.

Then the young May felt the old crone go limp in her arms. The poor thing had died quietly in her sleep.

When she awoke, May was crying softly. It took her some time to gather herself before she could stand and move about. She went to the edge of the lake and splashed some cool water on her eyes. Then she looked down at her own reflection. With a sigh, she saw her white feathers and her stooped posture.

Out of the corner of her eye she caught the reflection of a white butterfly. She jerked her head up just in time for the gossamer creature to land on her bill.

"Are you going to follow me as you once did," the butterfly asked in a whisper of a voice. "Will you now go where I lead?"

"Am I still dreaming?" May asked.

The butterfly batted its wings and produced a gust of wind worthy of a summer storm. "No," it said. "You have finally awakened."

May considered. "Yes," she said. I will follow wherever you go."

So the butterfly led her to a field where all the geese and their goslings were settled. Young mothers struggled to entertain their children as they prepared for the long journey to the south.

The butterfly settled in the middle of a circle of young birds. May followed and sat beside it. The butterfly flitted up to rest on her shoulder.

"Rock me," cried a little girl. "Momma's too busy. Will you rock me?"

"No me," shouted another.

"Tell us a story," honked a young boy.

Without thinking twice, May gathered up the little ones and began to rock them and croon. The butterfly began to whisper in her ear the most beautiful story, which she repeated word-for-word to the children.

So it was that May became the storyteller and caretaker of the little ones. The butterfly would always appear on her shoulder to tell her new tales to pass on.

Two geese happening upon this scene one afternoon were moved to discuss what they saw.

"Isn't that old May," one said. "I thought she hated children."

The other said, "Oh my goodness no. She has changed entirely. You will never see her alone again. They flock to her. She is so beloved by all the little ones that we have taken to calling her Mother Goose."

The Depths of Charity

In a clear blue sea that sparkled like a basket of sapphires there lived a sleek gray dolphin named Mangrove. Of all the creatures in the sea, Mangrove was heralded as the most self-less. It was an image he worked hard to keep.

"My reputation shall exist long after I am gone. I shall live forever in the minds of others," he thought.

This is not to say that he was not giving. Mangrove was always first to donate to the poor. He ran charity committees and organized drives for those in need. Mangrove was on every board of directors, solid citizen and model mammal.

Unfortunately, Mangrove was keenly aware of just how good a dolphin he was. He also had a very strict set of standards that those in need had to live up to in order to obtain his largesse.

"What in the undersea world are we giving kelp to that fellow for?" he demanded of his fellow do-gooders at their weekly meeting. "He's been here before, hasn't he? Well, we never give twice to the same party. Strike his name and tell him to get off the dole."

His fellow committee members were not shocked by

73

this outburst. They all knew that Mangrove's standards were stringent. He was kind to the point of being cruel.

"If anyone could kill someone with kindness, it is Mangrove," thought Tarpon.

He only thought it, though. He would never voice such a thing for fear of being ostracized. After all, being on all his committees had made Mangrove a very powerful dolphin. When he clicked and squealed, people listened.

"Tarpon," Mangrove bellowed. "Did you get the list of donations for the displaced manatees?"

Tarpon nearly shed his massive scales in his haste to find the file among his papers.

"Here it is," Tarpon said. "I had the plants sent out on the first wave this morning. They should be sitting down to sup on them as we speak."

You could hear plankton drop as Mangrove rounded on Tarpon.

"Sent out? Sent out! How dare you presume to usurp my authority in these matters?" The dolphin fumed. "Nothing is ever sent out until the media have been assembled to witness the giving. Never."

Tarpon must have been feeling like the fighting fish he was, for in that moment, he decided to tread water and not back down.

"They were starving," Tarpon said in a clear, firm voice. "The red tide killed all the food, and many of them are sick and starving. They couldn't wait so much as a moment longer. It was the right thing to do."

The silence at the meeting erupted into a series of murmurs and nodding.

Realizing that public opinion was turning against him, Mangrove decided to change his tack.

"Of course," he said. "You are right Mr. Tarpon. We should have been more aware of their needs. Let's move on to the subject of the street urchins in our midst."

And so it went for the rest of that meeting, and in many others like it. Mangrove went on doing what good he thought his fellow creatures deserved. In the process, he was given many accolades by the community.

Time passed, and Mangrove became an old dolphin. Feeling that he had earned it, he took a vacation to the islands. He had aided those living in that often storm-ravaged region.

It was a beautiful place. Whenever he did go there, he was sure to stay in the finest five-star lodging. He always took the direct route, never stopping to visit the quaint little villages along the way.

This time he had heard of a place where he was very nearly worshipped for his great acts of kindness. He had read about the little place in one of the many glowing articles about him.

"I shall go down there and give them the thrill of their lives," he thought. "Also, I shall see how my money is being spent."

So it came to pass that Mangrove was in the waters just off the coast of the Isle of Worth when the first big storm of the season hit. There had been no sign of the massive tropical storm building so near his destination, and Mangrove was taken completely by surprise.

Not so young and strong as he once was, Mangrove was tossed like flotsam in a whirlpool. Debris from the human world beat him. As the storm's fury was spent, he was rolled up onto the white sand beach. He was stranded.

Alone and in pain, he opened his aching eyes to scan the shore. The first sight that met his eyes was a white pelican.

The bird cocked its head and peered intently at him.

"So you're not dead." The bird sighed. "Just as well. You're too big a fish for me anyhow."

"Mustering his pride, Mangrove retorted, "I am a mammal, sir, not a fish."

The pelican chuckled. "I'll be sure and make that fine distinction to the vultures when they arrive."

Seeing the flash of panic in Mangrove's eyes, the pelican took pity on him.

"Oh, all right. I'll go alert the rescue brigade."

Soon Mangrove felt a tug on his tail. Fearing the vultures, he slapped frantically to keep the attacker away.

"Shhhhh, now," called a dolphin voice from behind him. "It's only the rescue squad here to get you into the water before you bake out here when the sun comes out."

So he was pulled and prodded until he was back in the water. He was helped by a rag-tag group of creatures ranging from sea slugs to clown fish. They towed him to a part of the coral reef where an aid station was set up.

He was tended and given some kelp broth. It took days for him to heal and, as he did, he began to get to know the creatures that had rescued him. There was a three-armed sea star, a manatee with propeller marks on its back, urchins of every size and shape, and a pod of dolphins.

They had very little food and few worldly goods, but they ministered to his needs and always fed him the best of what they had. He was given the biggest section of the reef in which to dwell. They never seemed to tire of tending to his wounds or sharing their meager rations.

One day he watched as a caravan of dolphins brought in the relief packages from his very own organization. Realizing that this would be a very opportune moment to reveal his identity, Mangrove swam over to the unloading area.

Crate after crate of goods were opened. They were filled with all sorts of food and medical supplies. As he got closer, he heard two groupers chatting.

"Thanks be to that wonderful fish," said one. "Without Mr. Tarpon, we would all have perished after this last storm."

Stung by these words, Mangrove seethed. "Why that no good, two-timing Tarpon," he muttered to himself. "He's taken all the credit for my good works!"

He was about to interrupt the chat when he was brought up short by what he heard.

"That awful Mangrove had us struck off the aid list because he said we had suffered too many storms and were draining their resources," said the other grouper. "If it weren't for Tarpon's brilliant idea to talk to those media fish and sing the old dolphin's praises, we would never have this help today.

That Tarpon deserves a medal."

Had he done what the grouper said? Could he have been so cruel?

Yes, he thought. He had been a fool. To him the ones he was helping were not real beings, but a means to an end. He had enjoyed the popularity and power.

The scales fell from his eyes and he knew what he had to do.

"Ahem," he said, attracting the attention of all those in the unloading area.

"It appears that I have a confession to make."

Intrigued, they all crowded around.

"I am that awful dolphin these groupers have spoken of.

Instantly there was a thrashing around him and a flood of apologies from the groupers.

"Never apologize for being right," he told the fish. "Tarpon does deserve a medal, and I was a fool. I am so sorry for the way I have treated my fellow creatures in the name of charity."

He had come this far, he thought, and so he chose to go all the way to confess his shortcomings.

"While I was doing some good, I still saw those in need as being inferior," he said. "I thought that because I had not suffered from poverty or disaster, I was somehow above you. Because I had been spared, I thought I was better than those who were smitten. I thought that those who were worthy, as I thought myself to be, would be spared the fury of the sea. I know now that I was wrong."

Now he broke down entirely. "I have seen through your kindness and selfless acts that you are the best of all creatures and that your loss was merely an inexplicable act of nature. Please, forgive me."

They all gathered around him. Some nodded their approval; others gave him a reassuring pat on the back.

Not long after that, Mangrove returned home. He resigned all his lofty posts and put Tarpon in charge. Instead of organizing, he chose to spend his remaining years out among his fellow sea-dwellers. He set out to do good as just one creature among many.

His actions were small—a smile, a helping hand to a neighbor, the gift of a hot meal to a hungry stranger.

Whenever anyone asked his name or offered to repay him, he said, "I am no one. I am everyone. Don't give back to me. When it is your turn, give to the next one in need."

That was how the old dolphin learned that it is better to live long in others' hearts than in their minds.

The Crab

In the shallows by a jetty of large gray rocks lived a fiddler crab named Clack. He was so named for the sound his pinchers made every time someone passed his way. While the other Fiddlers spent their time skittering hither and yon and playing their tunes, Clack remained silent. His music was disharmony and the pleas of the other crabs for him to change his tune fell upon deaf ears.

Backed into his hole Clack kept a constant vigil. When anyone passed too close to his front door they would be lucky to escape with just a good scare, as his large claw darted out and clacked shut at them.

It didn't matter if it was friend or foe. Clack gave the same greeting to all that passed. He simply snapped at them.

Odd thing was that, deep down, Clack was a very tender sort of fellow who wanted nothing more than to have friends and loved ones about him. He longed to show off his collection of flotsam and exchange the latest news as the others did.

Unfortunately, it was his nature to snap and pinch. If there was music in his heart he certainly didn't hear it over all the harsh words he drummed up.

Whenever his old friend Puffer fish swam up to say hello, Clack would say the most surly things that came to mind, such as, "Looking portly today aren't we Puffie? Looking fit to be caught at any moment."

Although Puffer knew his friend never meant what he said he still felt a little prickle under his scales. He wondered how anyone could be happy making others feel discomfort.

Clack knew how to be nice. He had seen it done often enough. Somehow he just couldn't bring himself to say the sweet thing when the sour caused such a pleasant stir.

"Besides," he said to himself. "They all know that I am only joking. Just trying to liven things up. If they can't take a joke they deserve to feel the pinch."

Well time passed and after a few years of what Clack considered to be his witty remarks he was surprised to find that he was lonely.

"Why," he asked himself. "It just doesn't add up? I'm the life of the party. Yet here I am every Saturday night without a place to go. I haven't been to a party in ages."

So Clack decided it must be the neighborhood. That was it of course. He would just pick himself up and scuttle off to someplace where he was appreciated.

Clack moved. He settled. He Clacked and wisecracked. He told the local starfish that they were too pointy headed to have any sense. He clipped the fin of a prominent cod and scraped at the coral whenever he could.

Clack moved again. He settled again. And again. And again.

"The world is such a terrible place," he complained to all who would listen. "Creatures have no sense of humor. Their values are all wrong. If everyone were easy-going like me, things would be great."

More often than not he found himself telling these things to himself, as he was alone in his hole.

Then one day he met a young crab that was playing among the anemone. The young crab looked up to Clack and admired the way he fast-talked everyone. The little fellow thought to himself, "Someday I will run everyone around with an iron claw just like Clack."

So it came to pass that the happy young crab stopped playing happily with the clown fish. His games of hide and seek among the anemone ended as well. Clack watched in dismay as the young crab became an outcast among his peers.

The little crab dug his hole just like Clack's and secreted himself away there.

Well, this had to stop, Clack thought, and he scuttled over to the other hole.

"Boy," he bellowed. "Get your crabby self on out here."

Hearing his hero's voice the young crab rushed out.

"What in the ocean and tide pool has gotten into you," Clack demanded. "You used to be a happy young fellow. Now every time I look over here you're harassing some poor citizen, poking at folks and being generally surly."

Stunned, the young crab replied, "But I only wanted to be tough like you."

"Tough? I'm not tough. I'm a funny guy. I make people laugh. Everybody loves me," he said. But he had a tickling feeling at the back of his shell that he always got when there was something bad about to happen.

The young crab couldn't have been more hurt or disillusioned. Here was his hero, the crab of steel, acting like a simpering old fool. He was so angry that he lashed out at Clack and the two were soon kicking up a cloud of dust and locked in mortal combat.

When the sand settled the young crab had won the battle and scuttled back to his hole. Clack had lost his right claw, but was able to make it back to his hole.

Once inside he began to seriously ponder his life. As painful as it was to admit, he had been wrong. His scathing sense of humor, his snappish ways and his unyielding sense of what was right and wrong had made him an outcast.

Worse, he had unwittingly lured a young crab away from the right path. He knew what he must now do. He had led by poor example before and now he must lead by good. He would have to come out of his hole and greet other creatures with a smile instead of a scowl.

It dawned on him that what he really needed to make things right was his big claw back so that he could play a tune and draw the other crab out.

Then Clack did something he had never done before. He scuttled to shore and looked up at the stars. "Please," he said to the night sky. "Please let my claw grow back so that I may put things to rights. I promise never to use it to snap at anyone ever again."

There was no answer. Clack scuttled back to his hole and went to sleep.

When he awoke he found that his claw had grown back good as new. He rushed out of the hole. "Thank you," he said. "I know what I have to do."

He went to the mouth of the young crab's hole and for the first time in his life he made music. It was so strong and beautiful that creatures gathered around him to listen. The tune ran a long course starting out rough and clipped, just as he had once been. Then it became lonely and sad. Finally the music soared like the gulls above the surface.

When he finished all was quiet. The young crab moved ever so slowly out of his hole.

"I want to make music like that," he sighed, forgetting to be tough. "Teach me how."

Clack scuttled over and rested his claw on the young crab's back.

"There are some songs young fellow that cannot be taught," he said. "They have to be earned."

"Get out of that hole and go out into the world boy. Listen more than you talk. Smile more than you frown. Hold yourself back and don't snap," Clack added. "Then maybe your song can begin the way mine ended. If it does the world will be your oyster."

Soul Food

awn broke over the Arctic and the water was alive with the splashing of hundreds of seals. It was time once again for Ceylon to perform her daily tasks. She was a very reliable young harp seal and took on a great many responsibilities.

"Why I vow that girl works harder than any bull," said one of the local matrons. "She takes on everything that comes her way."

"Too true," barked another stout seal on the rocky beach. "She is a marvel."

All the seals on the beach clapped their flippers in approval as Ceylon towed in a line strung with herring. They barked and rolled when she herded a large group of furry white pups to their swimming lessons.

Ceylon was glad to have the praise of her fellows. She was happy to help the other seals by watching their young pups and gathering extra food for the old and infirm.

Unfortunately, her efforts were never their own reward. Never was Ceylon satisfied with her day's work or herself. She was forever hungry for more. More praise, more work, more food. More food.

"I am tired," she said to herself. "I must eat to keep up my strength."

"I am celebrating," she said to herself, and took a third helping of cod.

So it went, when she was nervous, afraid, angry or lonely, Ceylon would experience a gnawing hunger that would send her out to hunt and eat.

It was a big hole Ceylon was filling, a hole that was not part of her body, but of her soul.

As the years passed Ceylon began to expand from all her voracious needs. Her once sleek form became bloated and lumpy. Her attitude suffered as well. She became withdrawn. Ceylon became desperately aware of her appearance and refused invitations from her friends to lie on the ice pack and sun herself.

"What is wrong with her," the matrons asked each other. "Why won't she come out of the water?"

"Perhaps we have offended her," one said. "We rely on her too much. We should lighten her load, poor thing."

So they tried to take away some of her burdens, but it only made her worse. "Do you think I am too old and fat to do my job anymore," she barked. "I can do twice as much now. My size does not matter."

Oh, but it did. Her friends did not think less of her, but she was unable to accept herself.

She swam away as fast as she could, and cried her salty tears into the ocean.

Ceylon swam to a desolate flo of ice and slid herself up onto the white, snowy embankment. She looked up at the sky and out over the wide, cold sea.

"I hate them all," she shouted. "They do not appreciate me. Nobody loves me. I am all alone."

Just then the sky began to light and burn with colors that seemed to swim in the air like a million ghostly bright seals. The Northern Lights filled the sky.

"Oh," Ceylon gasped. "Aurora! Hear me and grant my prayer. Make me thin and young again that I may know true happiness."

The lights grew brighter than she had ever seen them. In a flash they engulfed her.

"Granted," the lights said. "That you may learn."

When the light was gone Ceylon looked at herself and saw a sleek young body. "Thank you," she called and dove into the sea.

She swam back to the others as quickly as she could. Everyone greeted her warmly.

"Feeling better my dear," asked an old one. "You are looking well."

"Oh yes," Ceylon said. "I am wonderful now. I am back to my old self."

Once again Ceylon took on her tasks. Once again they all sang her praises and once again she was empty. Less than a year passed before she was back to her old unwieldy size.

"I must swim back to the flo and ask Aurora to save me again," she said to herself. And so she did.

Once on the ice she called out to the heavens. "Please help me, I beg you."

The sky filled with the swimming colors of Aurora and

again the voice spoke. "You cannot get your fill," it said. "You do not crave food for the body, but for the spirit. Only when you have filled your heart will your body be satisfied and your life be whole."

Panicked at the prospect of not being magically cured Ceylon wept. "I don't know how to do what you ask," she cried. "Please, just fix me as you did before."

"I will do better than to fix your body," the voice said. "I will heal you instead. Gaze upon me now. Look deep and see the light."

Ceylon did not care what it took. She only wanted to be changed for good and all, so she did as she was told.

Looking up at the dancing rays she began to feel changed, softened, opened to something new.

"Please," she said. "I think I asked for the wrong wish last time. I think I should have asked you to grant me peace. My vanity was too strong. I asked for something outward when the pain is inside of me."

The lights burst from the sky and enveloped her once again. She felt warmth and freedom and a joy she had only imagined. When the light faded she was left with its glow inside her.

Looking down she saw herself as she had been before. Portly, older, strong, soft and whole, was what she saw. She liked what she saw. She loved what she felt.

When at last she returned to the others everyone noticed the change that had been wrought.

"My dear child," said the old one. "You look positively radiant."

Another said, "I have never seen you more healthy and happy. It is nothing short of miraculous."

A gaggle of younger seals crowded around her. "Ceylon," one said. "You must tell us your secret."

Ceylon smiled at them all. "It is called the Soul Food Diet. You get to eat all you want of the bread of life. Drink your fill of the milk of kindness, and for dessert you taste the sweetness of your life. It is very fulfilling."

Looking Up

wo clouds drifted high in the sky on a balmy afternoon. They were horsetail clouds, stretching out across the stratosphere and looking down on the world.

One said to the other, "It is wonderful to be our type of cloud."

The other agreed. They had started out as thick clouds until the wind had run across them like a brush streaking through white paint.

The land spread out beneath them, and they could see as their shadows passed across the plains.

Far off on the horizon they could see a front beginning to build. The ceiling of the sky got darker with other clouds gathering for a rally. They sighed, for they knew this would result in a rally of their own.

Soon there would be a lot of shouting and rumbling, ending in tears to drench humanity.

"Here we go again," said the first horsetail cloud. "I really don't like those dark clouds gathering that way."

The other cloud cast a glance toward the groups of darker and heavier clouds that drifted past, heading for the larger group.

"Hmmm," the second said. "I tend to agree. Perhaps we ought to gather some of our own to keep us company. I hate the thought of being just us two amid a rough crowd like that."

So they gathered the cirrus and nimbus and others of the light and lithe crowd into conference.

They called a meeting to order as the distant sky began to rumble.

"I vote that we keep them out of our part of the sky," said one large bank of cloud that resembled an ice cream sundae.

"I don't think we can keep them out," retorted a wisp. "We tried it before in my part of the country and failed miserably. Perhaps we could come to an agreement of taking turns on alternate days."

There was a loud crack and a whiff of ozone as two impatient puffs, shaped like twin gavels, banged on a tabletop cloud.

"Order," one gavel cried. "We must simply learn to tolerate the dark clouds' presence among us. Just ignore them. Pretend they don't exist. Eventually they will get bored and move on."

This seemed a sensible suggestion, and so it was agreed to ignore the newcomers.

The white clouds were all well pleased with themselves until they realized that the other clouds' meeting had broken up some time ago and that they were not only on the move, but almost upon them.

Just as all the clouds came together the wind began to

howl. "Don't leave me out," it wailed. "I'm a mover and a shaker, just like all of you."

"No, absolutely not," cried the first horsetail cloud. "Dark clouds are bad enough. We'll have no wind mixing into this debate."

"At least that's one thing we can all agree on," said the deep voice of a dark thunderhead. "Be off with you now wind."

Just as the thunderhead and the horsetail were about to charge at the wind they bumped together. The sky split with lightning as a result.

"Oh just what we needed," muttered the second horse-tail cloud.

But it was too late. The wind began to blow and the clouds, now packed together, began to rumble. Flashes of lightning rattled like sabers in an ancient war. The tears fell in torrents.

One spiteful remark led to another and soon one cloud gave another the cold shoulder until a hail of insults pelted the ground.

For hours and hours the battle raged, long into the night. Bodies clashed, and their life's blood was wrung out. In the pitch black of night it was impossible to tell one combatant from another. When dawn broke the sky was clear without a cloud of any kind in sight.

The blue sky looked down upon the ground and called to the sun who trained its gaze upon what was now an ocean.

"Gone and done it now haven't they," the sky commented to the sun.

"Indeed they've really mixed it up," the sun said. "Hello down there. Can anybody hear me?"

The sea roared with all the clouds' voices. They had been reduced to their elemental form and mashed together in one blue-green sea.

The sun made a command decision and began to burn as brightly as it could. A fog rose from the waters. It rose and thickened and then floated upward. After many exhausting hours the sun backed off enough to allow the fog to form back into clouds.

Every size and shape cloud emerged from the gray mist. Every one was new and different from what it had once been.

When they were all assembled the sky asked, "Well children. Are we all still angry this morning?"

For the life of them the clouds could not find a reason to be upset. They all felt confused and a bit jumbled. Somehow that dunking and mingling together for one night has washed away their differences.

"Excuse me," said a small fluffy cloud that rather resembled a rose. "I think that maybe we can't be mad anymore because it would appear that we are all really made of the same water. Well, after all, it seems we only looked different."

The sun beamed at the little rosy cloud. "Well said little one. You have all come from the same place and no matter how you look or where you gather you are all destined to return to the same place. You will gather there again as one. So it makes little sense to live in such strife."

"The sky and wind and I have all agreed that we shall do this renewal on a regular basis so as to remind us all of where we come from and where we are bound."

And so they parted that fine morning. Some would still refuse to see the light and so were destined to cause more turmoil in the skies in which they lived.

But there were others, many others, who had learned to live in a sort of artistic harmony. They gathered daily in peace to paint the sky with hope for a better tomorrow.

IN THE END

The Spirited Horse

he grass was green and sweet when Maxwell the horse was a young colt trotting about the meadow. The birds sang the young horse's praises as he galloped across hill and dale, carrying his rider like a feather on the wind.

Aaaah, those had been the days. The world had been a clean and golden place for him.

"Max," came the shout that broke his reverie. "Get up you old sack of bones before I sell you for glue."

The man had grown old with Max, and his patience had gone along with his memory. The man no longer recalled the rollicking good times they had had together. Instead of looking back on his youth with fondness, he looked back in bitterness.

Max was not a reminder of his championship wins, nor his lithe and graceful salad days. No. To the man Max was a cruel reminder of his own aging. Because he hated himself for aging, so did he hate his old companion for showing the signs of their advancing years.

The old horse groaned and shook off the night's rest. Then he prepared himself for the day's work. Gone were the days of respect. Now he was put to all the lowliest of menial tasks. He was given the bare minimum of food and water. No sugar cubes hidden in flannel pockets or carrots offered after a good show. His stall was mucked out only occasionally. It was no longer the big stall, but was instead the small and rickety one with the squeaky hinges.

Max was not so much bitter as he was downtrodden. He didn't hate the man for hating him, but his hope was all but gone. Instead of looking forward to the day, he only marked it off in his mind as being one day closer to the end.

Today, however, Max knew there would be some excitement around the paddock because there was a new mount coming to join the stables. Blaze, a fine horse, had been bought just a few days earlier and would arrive today.

When the truck drove up, towing the horse trailer, all was bustle and activity around the stalls. Blaze, a lean, black stallion with a white streak running down his nose, stepped neatly and calmly down the ramp. He held his head high, knowing that he was a great horse. As he was led to his stall the horses whinnied a friendly greeting, but he was too great to answer.

Blaze had always been a nose faster than his siblings and friends. His lines were longer, smoother, and his easy grace seemed a gift not bestowed on any other horse for generations. Blaze was great and he knew it. His blood sang in his veins when it came his turn to show. He felt a power in his own being that gave him pride in himself. Perhaps just a bit too much pride.

The man beamed at his new acquisition. Although he

was not fit enough to ride the horse, his daughter, an excellent horsewoman, would do the training.

"Well, well, you are a fine one aren't you," the man said as he pulled a lump of sugar from his pocket and offered it to Blaze. "Settle in now son. Tomorrow we begin the serious business of training you for show."

Blaze watched with solemn eyes as the man welcomed him. Then his solemn look turned to confusion as he heard the man's harsh words to Max. Confusion gave way to unease when he saw the man jerk cruelly on the old horse's bridle.

After the people had gone the horses began to settle down for the night.

Max did his best to make him welcome.

He shuffled to the gate of his stall and called to Blaze, "You work hard young fellow. Do your best and make us all proud. When I look at you I see myself. I look forward to watching you train, so I can live a little longer through you."

"Be kind to the girl who will train you as she has always been good to me, even in my old age and decline she has continued to treat me with respect and love."

Now Blaze took the old horse's words more to heart that Max had intended. He knew that if Max had once been a prized show pony and was now a beaten-down relic in a sour-smelling stall, this was likely to be his fate as well.

Blaze began to fret over his fate. "If he made an error would the man strike him? Would he not be brushed and cared for?"

Blaze wanted to ask these questions of Max but was too proud. He worried instead and held it all inside until he felt terribly ill.

He paced and nickered and felt as if the walls were closing in around him. As dawn broke he was a skittish bundle of nerves. Then he saw a little boy standing before him in the stall.

The child was tiny, made more so by the imposing presence of the horse. Yet, for some reason, the child seemed unafraid.

The boy reached out and patted Blaze and the horse calmed instantly. "No fear now," said the child, and although he was far below him the voice sounded as if it were being spoken directly into Blaze's ear.

"You don't need fear now," the child said. "Save your fear for when you need it."

Blaze knelt down to look at the boy. He couldn't have been more than four years old, with hair like honey in the sunlight and bright green eyes.

"How can I need fear," the horse asked. Blaze had always believed that strong horses tamped down their emotions. Emotions were useless thing that only got in the way. He was ashamed of his fear.

The boy explained that emotions were like tools, to be taken out and used to build your character. "We must all feel fear and anger if we are to feel love and joy. So far, you have felt a great deal of pride and very little else."

"Now you need to take out your fear and show it to the man," he said. "When he comes today I want you to show him your feelings about how he treats old Max. Don't try to be brave and hide how you feel. It is only a form of deception, and deception does not serve you well."

At that moment there was the sound of the stable doors opening and a shaft of sunlight pierced the dark stalls and blinded Blaze for a moment. When his eyes adjusted, the child was gone.

The man and his daughter arrived. As soon as the man reached for the bridle, Blaze reared back his hooves slicing the air.

"Woa, now," the man said. "A little spirited this morning aren't we?"

He reached again for the bridle, but Blaze showed such terror at his touch that the man stepped back and allowed his daughter to try her hand.

Seeing the young woman, Blaze remembered Max's endorsement of her and allowed her to lead him calmly from the stall. He worked well with the girl, but from the training paddock he could see Max being yanked and tugged and browbeaten by the man.

When he saw this he stopped abruptly and then raced to the gate. He reared and whinnied and pounded the ground, drawing the man's attention. The man ran over, alarmed that something was amiss with his prized animal. He narrowly avoided the flying hooves.

Confused and angry the man left Blaze with his daughter and went back to Max. He was so absorbed in the puzzle over Blaze's attitude that he forgot to be angry with Max.

This happened over and over again in varying situations until, by the end of a week, the man was beside himself with grief.

"Why should you hate me so," The man shouted at Blaze after another bout. "What have I ever done to you but shown you kindness and feed you well."

He could hardly believe the insanity of this new horse. It appeared to the man that every time he took Max out for some work Blaze ran amuck.

Max trotted up to the man and nuzzled at the pocket where he kept the sugar. The man swatted at Max and instantly Blaze reared and let out a piercing cry.

"It's Max," the man said. "He doesn't like Max!"

"No," said a small voice from beside him. "He doesn't like what you do to Max. He fears that you will treat him the same way."

Shocked beyond words with this revelation the man looked down and saw the small boy.

"Max has never harmed you, because he felt compassion for you," said the boy. "He knew you were in a kind of torment far worse than what you inflicted upon him. In Blaze you see what you were and in Max you see what you have become. But you have no one to blame for beating you down but yourself."

The man's mind ran back over the week's events and he saw with perfect clarity that the child was right. When he looked down to tell him so the child was gone. In a panic the man whirled around looking for the child, but he had vanished.

"Father are you all right," his daughter asked.

The man reached over and took the bridle of his old horse. "I haven't been very good to you these past years have I old man?"

Max shook his head.

"Well, if it is any consolation, I haven't been too good to myself," he added.

He reached into his pocket and pulled out three cubes of sugar. The first he offered to Max. The second he gave to Blaze. Then he took the third and popped it into his mouth.

He let the sugar melt on his tongue and remembered being a boy. Suddenly he knew that life could be sweet again.

The goodness was there for the taking, for himself and to share with old friends and new.

He decided it was time to taste life again. And so he did.

Swan Lake

Of all the creatures who lived in and around the lake the most envied was the swan. Her graceful ways and gleaming white feathers captured the attention of all who beheld her.

"I hate that bird," grumbled the Mallard. "She thinks that we should all pay attention to her because she is so majestic, so grand. Well, I for one can not stand the way she puts on airs."

There was a chorus of chirps and a flutter of speculation among the other birds that had gathered by the water's edge.

Just then, Swan glided close to where the other birds were gathered and inclined her head in welcome. "The water is fine today," she commented. "Care to come in for a dip?"

Mallard nearly molted at the perceived insult. Puffed with righteous indignation Mallard waddled to the water's edge and impolitely declined the offer.

Swan shrugged and glided off to the far side of the lake. None of the others noticed her shoulders hunching, her bill drop closer to her breast or how deliberately she paddled to get away.

Mallard huffed away and began anew with her audience, "Oh she'd like that wouldn't she, Miss Fancy Feathers," she spat. "Love to have us swim behind her to make her look even more grand. Love to have us all follow adoringly and pay court."

All brown and black striped feathers, short neck and bad temper; Mallard paced. That miserable swan had plagued her for months by merely existing in her circle of influence. Mallard had been the community leader before that. It had been she who gathered food for the homeless animals who came to the meadow from the cities. Mallard had been the best at telling exciting tales of the hunting season.

Worst of all was the fact that when she was beside Swan, Mallard felt changed. She had always been kind, happy, the salt of the Earth, until Swan glided into her life. Now the salt that she was became so harsh it corroded everything she touched.

No matter how hard she tried Mallard could not manage a single kind word to spare the glamorous white vision of the lake.

Meanwhile, Swan was in despair. When she first came to the pond she had taken a liking to Mallard and her sense of humor, her flair. She had been so lonely since her mate had died from a stone hurled by a careless boy. She had been left with a nest full of eggs and no one to provide for her.

Every day she would do her best to preen herself and then coast along the little piers where people gathered to watch the water. She greedily hoarded the crumbs tossed to her and brought them back to her nest and her newly hatched chicks.

She had hoped to ask the Mallard for help at first, but was driven off by her anger.

So time passed, and Swan became weaker and thinner from exhaustion and loneliness. Her feathers became dull and her eyes clouded with fear.

Every day that passed gave Mallard more satisfaction. Finally the news came one day that Swan had passed away.

"A terrible discovery it was," chattered the squirrel. "She'd had a nest hidden away and filled with hungry chicks. Poor thing just worked herself to death."

Upon hearing this revelation the blood in Mallard's veins ran cold with dread. Had she been wrong? Had her own low self-esteem, her vanity, stood in the way of Swan's getting the help she needed? She knew the answer was yes, and in that moment the other birds knew the part she had played in the beautiful bird's demise.

She was now an outcast. Alone she waded away into the lake and paddled off to a far corner to brood.

"What have I done," she said aloud to the empty place she had chosen.

To her surprise the water itself gave her the answer saying in a deep and echoing voice, "You have disappointed me."

Mallard trembled in terror. The water, always around her, supporting her, feeding her, slaking her thirst, had never before uttered sound. Now it spoke in a voice so sorrowful she wept the harder for having heard it.

Wait, she thought, no one she knew had ever heard it speak. Surely she was overwrought and imagining.

"Yes," it said, reading her thoughts. "I can speak, but not to your ears. I speak to your heart."

Still frightened she said, "Why haven't I heard you before?"

"Your heart was deaf to me," it said. "You blocked me out the day you began to hear the anger and the fear."

Mallard knew this was true, but was not able to let go of her pride. "Swan should have asked for help," she pouted. "She was too proud to come to little me for help."

The water began to churn around her, "Yes, you are small, but not in size Mallard. You have diminished yourself with your envy."

"Swan saw you for what was inside and liked you, while you saw only the exterior and found hate."

Hearing this Mallard broke. She cried and cried adding her tears to the great body of the lake. "I am worthless. I give up. I should just walk to the fox's den and get my life over with."

Now the water calmed. "There is a better way to end your life of anger and self-loathing than in death," the water said. "Wade to the middle of me and then dive as far down as you can. Then let out all of your breath as you come back to the surface. With each puff of air you release, picture your anger and hate floating away to my surface."

"I will surely drown," wailed the duck.

The water rippled as the lake let out a small chuckle. "No, I will not let you drown in me. I will only cleanse you of your fear and hate, and when you surface you can begin your new life."

For no reason she would ever be able to explain, Mallard believed. She swam to the center and dove. As she turned and began her ascent, releasing all her precious air and anger she could see the sun shining through the water. Shafts of light pierced the dark body of water and seemed to draw her toward their source.

Mallard broke the surface and lay prone on the water for some time until she got her wind back.

She heard the babbling of the other birds nearby and opened her eyes. A bevy of swan chicks gathered around her and moved her to shore.

"Have you seen our mother," one asked.

Looking back to the center of the lake she shook her head and replied, "No, but I have seen the place where she went and it is beautiful. I will care for you now, with some help from the lake."

Panicked, one chick cried, "Help from the lake? It's just a lake, how can it help anyone?"

Drawing the chick under her wing she smiled, "Sit down my child and let me tell you a story."

The Stone Carrier

On an island in the sea there was a small village. In this village each person had a task to perform in accordance with their gift.

Jacob was a Sweep because he was good at cleaning up other people's messes. Truman was a Boat Builder for he was good at calming the waters around him.

Alva's job was to be a Tender of animals, for he was good at keeping everyone together and would always look out for those who strayed.

Then there was Maya. She was a Stone Carrier, and this is her story.

When Maya was a girl she was the most sensitive child in the village. All who met her were sure she would grow up to be a Listener, for her perception was keen.

The role of Listener was very highly regarded in the village, for everyone needed the services one had to offer.

Maya had a gift for listening to what people said to each other and then helping them to understand each other. This was necessary because people did not always say what they really meant and so needed constant interpretation.

"My, what a lovely dress you have on my dear," said by a woman to another whom she disliked really meant something entirely different. It meant, "I wish I looked that good," or "I hope you fall into a puddle of mud."

Also, a man could say to his mate, "I am listening," when he meant to say, "I am not interested enough in what you are saying to pay attention, but do not wish to hurt your feelings."

Sometimes, people would even say, "I hate you," when they really meant, "I love you."

Oh it was a very complicated calling that Maya had inherited, and she knew it. She worked hard to do her best.

As part of her training she was told that she would have to step away from her own emotions.

"You must not get yourself all churned up inside. You are too sensitive for your own good. In order to help others," her professor had said, "you must not take offense too easily. Also you must not begin reading too much into what people tell you."

Try as she might, Maya could not stop feeling things. When people fought she felt angry. When they cried, she wept with them. When someone said things to be hurtful she felt the pain for those around her. She not only listened, she heard.

"Maya," her professor said, "I have a cure for your emotional attachment."

He handed her a large, sturdy, canvas sack with a shoulder strap.

"Every time you are about to feel hurt by something

someone says to you I want you to take a rock from the ground and put it in this sack," he advised. "At the end of the day I want you to take the sack and empty it into the sea."

This seemed a splendid solution to Maya, and so she took the sack. For the first few days the plan worked well. She would talk to people and then go out and scour the village for rocks. She collected a rock for every slight and sharp word. Then she tossed them in a heap by the seaside.

After a week of collecting the rocks she was growing tired. She decided to wait a few days before making the long walk to the shore to dump the rocks.

The bag became heavier by the day, and she kept telling herself that it was time to unload them, but somehow she seemed unable to let them go.

Maya had taken to spending her evenings cataloging the stones. "I got this dark blue one after that man said my listening needed work," she said to herself. "This orange one was found after that horrible woman said my hair was too long."

Instead of ridding herself of the baggage, Maya had learned to cherish it. The weeks turned into months, and soon Maya stopped listening for others and only worked for herself. She spent hours listening to other people's words and seeking meanings that were deeper and sometimes darker.

Her back began to bend and she became gaunt and angry looking.

Her professor, missing her at class, sought her out. He was deeply saddened by what he found.

"Child, child," he moaned. "What have you done to yourself? Did I not tell you to throw the stones into the sea?"

Maya bristled. Did he think her a fool? Did he think she would always listen to him and do whatever he advised? She was a wise woman and had found a true calling as a Stone Carrier. She knew her business better than anyone. She would not be told what to do.

"Go away," she snapped. "I am a fine Stone Carrier, and I do not need your advice."

He shook his head. He never thought Maya could come to this. In a fit of guilt he tried to wrestle the bag from her, but to no avail. Then he tried reason.

"Look at them my dear," he said. "They are not worth keeping. You must go to the sea and pitch them before they weigh you down so far that you cannot function."

Maya considered his words. She had not forgotten how to listen, only had she put her gift aside. She knew he was speaking the truth. "I will go and do as you say."

Satisfied, her old professor went away.

Maya collected up all the stones and put them in her sack. She strapped it to her back and went to the sea.

It was getting on to evening and the sun was setting over the water. Long golden rays stretched toward her and she walked ankle-deep in the briny shore-break. The tide was coming in and she had little time to do her task.

"Still," she thought, "It won't hurt to give them all one last look."

She sat on a large flat rock and took her treasures out of her pack and laid them all lovingly before her. With each one she held Maya remembered the pain, the anger, the hurt. She knew that she was too attached to let them all go. She replaced them in her pack and turned to step off the rock and return home. It was too late.

The tide had come in and as Maya took the step she slipped and plunged into the deepening water. Though the sack on her back pinned her to the bottom she would not shrug it off. Within moments, Maya ceased her struggle and drowned.

To this day the people of her village remember the lesson they learned from the one-time Listener. The rock on which she had her last thoughts was taken from the shore and brought to the center of the village. There it was carved by the professor, a shaper of beings, into a statue of Maya.

The inscription on the base reads, "Here stands the Listener, sad and alone. The result of a woman who turned her heart to stone."

Joey's Healing Story

ometimes there are things that happen to us that change us. The change can be for better or worse.

In the case of a small kangaroo's life being changed, it was both.

Joey had always been a very kind and giving kangaroo. Although he was very poor, he always found something he could share with his friends and neighbors.

Sometimes Joey would share a joke, sometimes a bunch of leaves he had gathered that were especially tender.

One day, however, Joey's wife was terribly sick, and he was out looking for some special herbs to make her well. After hours of searching he finally found one tiny plant growing from a rock on a hillside.

He heard a voice behind him. "Please, could you share that with me," said a chubby little wombat. "My neighbor is very ill with the mange and that will cure him."

For the first time in his life, Joey did not give a thought to anyone else. "I am sorry, but this is all there is and I cannot spare any or else my mate might not get well."

Joey took off as fast as he could and the chubby little wombat could not keep up. However, Joey could hear wombat's pleas long after he was out of sight.

He rushed home and ground all of the plant into some water to make a healing broth. His mate became healthy and strong soon after taking the medicine.

Although Joey never saw the wombat again he was haunted by his decision not to help him. He had heard of the death of the wombat's neighbor and had decided never to tell anyone his terrible secret. It was certain his refusal to help had caused the death of the wombat's neighbor.

"I could have gone back out to search for more herbs after I had helped my mate," he thought bitterly. "I could have given him half and both could have recovered."

Days went by and then weeks and months. Joey spent all of his spare time doing as many good deeds for others as he could think of, but still his heart was heavy with sadness over what he had done so long ago.

With each day that he kept the secret locked in his heart it grew more painful, worse than a thistle stuck in his paw.

He was so angry with himself for his own mistake, that any time he saw another animal make an error he would be very hard and cruel to them.

For the most part, his friends thought he was the same, but inside he was cold and empty. He had changed.

Then one day he found a golden eagle caught in a hunter's snare. The great bird beat its majestic wings furiously, but could do nothing to free itself.

Quickly Joey hopped over and gnawed the ropes and tugged with his paws until the bird was free.

"Thank you my friend," said the bird. "You are truly a good neighbor and a kind soul."

With that Joey began to cry as he had never cried before. He could not help it. "No, no I am terrible—a beast!"

The bird covered Joey with his wing and Joey poured out the tale he had never told another living soul.

When he was done the eagle said, "I am sorry to tell you this Joey, but you are not a terrible beast. You are just an ordinary animal who made a mistake you could not change."

Joey cried, "I can not even ask wombat's neighbor to forgive me, because he is gone. I cannot make it right."

"Listen," the eagle said. "Having the one you harmed forgive you would only make you feel better for a short while. You must forgive yourself for your mistake."

Slowly, Joey stopped crying. He realized that just telling his terrible secret to this stranger had made him feel a bit better. Inside he began to feel warmer and more filled with good feelings than he had in years.

The thistle was out of his heart and he could begin now to heal his spirit.

He thanked the eagle and hopped off for home. Along the way he gathered some tender leaves for his mate and some for his neighbors.

Joey was a new kangaroo after that. Instead of criticizing others for their mistakes he comforted them. Instead of doing good deeds to settle his guilt, he did them because his heart was once again full of love for other creatures.

From then on, if he had a sorrow, he would confide his troubles in his mate or a friend.

He had learned that healing does not come from shame, anger or empty acts, but from an honest and open heart.

Searcher's Moving Experience

It was moving day, one of many in the life of Searcher Bear. He was a restless soul and so being needed to change his digs rather often.

"But Papa," said his little daughter, Sacha. "Why must I leave all my new friends? I don't want to be the new bear at school again this year. I want things to stay as they are."

The papa bear gave a bit of a grunt. "Things never stay the same, no matter how much you want them to," he said gruffly. "Better to change it yourself than have it sneak up and do you a mischief. Besides, if you want happiness, you have to go out and look for it."

As always, little Sacha bit her lip and said no more. Ever since her Mamma had gone away to live with the sky, her Papa had been different. He still loved her and hugged her, but now when he looked at her he seemed to be seeing something far away.

"My Papa is like my favorite jigsaw puzzle," she told her teacher one day. "Only he can't get all put together because Mama is the piece he is missing."

When her teacher heard this she gave Sacha a big bear hug.

117

That was two teachers ago, Sacha mused as she finished packing her little trunk. Two neighborhoods and too many friends ago to think about.

They moved to a new cave. It was very big and very nice, but Sacha didn't much care. She was learning not to get too attached to where she lived or whom she met.

It was a hard thing for her to do, so she invented a game. The picture game. When Mamma had gone away, all she had left were pictures in a scrapbook to remind her. So now, when she met someone new she would draw their picture and put it in a little book she made.

She found that if she could think of the places as books and the new bears she met as pictures in the books, then she could just close the book when it was time to leave and carry them all with her.

Unfortunately, Sacha became so comfortable with this system that she stopped actually meeting anyone. She would just sit under a tree or at her desk at school and sketch everyone and everything around her. She didn't talk to anyone, because she could not really write yet and so could not take their words and put them in her books.

"How was school today," Searcher asked one evening. Sacha shrugged.

"I haven't met any of your new friends yet," he said. "You should bring them to the cave and introduce them. I imagine you have many new playmates."

Sacha shrugged again. This was disturbing to Searcher. His little girl was never rude or disobedient. She was outgoing and happy, just like her mother. He brushed the thought of his beloved wife aside before it could hurt his heart some more.

"Sacha Hopewell Bear, I asked you a question and it is time for an answer," he demanded. "Who are your friends, and why have I not met them?"

Sacha looked away. What was she to tell her father? Should she tell him that all the friends she had were scattered over the earth like seeds, all growing without her? Should she tell him how lonely she was? Perhaps one day she would be bold and ask if he had any friends. It was a thing she often wondered about.

"We haven't been here very long Papa," she said instead. "I have been too busy with my school work and unpacking to meet too many friends. I will work on it."

This seemed to satisfy him, and he said, "Well, that's better. That wasn't such a hard thing to say now was it?" Oh, but it had been, for Sacha had never before lied to her father.

Time passed, and the Bears settled into their new home. But, as the close of the first year drew near, Searcher began to make plans to find a new home. He was relieved that for once, Sacha had not argued with him over their upcoming move.

Then came the call from the school. "Mr. Bear," said the Principal, "I am sorry to inform you that your daughter Sacha has been suspended from class for one week for fighting in the play yard."

If Searcher had not been sitting at the time he would surely have needed a chair at that moment. His little angel in a fight? It must be an error. If not an error, then he would get to the bottom of who would dare attack his child, for surely this must be what had happened.

Upon arriving at the principal's office he was greeted with a horrible sight. His baby was huddled in the arms of some lady bear and was weeping bitter tears. "Give it back! Give it back, back, back," she moaned.

He would kill whoever had brought her to this state. He could barely contain himself well enough to speak.

Before he could reach her, a teacher intercepted him. "Please come with me sir," she said.

He was having none of this. He would take his Sacha home, pack up and leave immediately. He knew he shouldn't have stayed here so long.

But the teacher was firm saying, "We must talk before you see your daughter." Moved by the seriousness of her tone, Searcher went with her.

"Mr. Bear," she said. "Have you met any of Sacha's friends?"

Puzzled and a bit miffed, he said, "No, I haven't."

"Would you like to meet them," the teacher said patiently.

Now he was really angry. Did she think him a bad father? "Of course I would," he snapped.

The teacher handed him a thick, hand-bound sheaf of papers. "Here they are," she said.

He snatched the book and began to leaf through the pages. He recognized his daughter's skillful drawings. He also recognized many of her old friends and some sketches of their various homes.

"Is this a joke," he asked.

"Sacha got into a terrible fight because one of the others took this book and began to look at the drawings. Sacha went wild and attacked. She thinks these pictures are real. She has substituted them for actual friends, because she is afraid of losing them when you move away."

No. This could not be true. He would take her away from all of this crazy talk. He threw the book into the trash basket by the desk. He stormed out of the office and pulled Sacha away from the one holding her. He carried her home.

Once they were home Searcher told her that they would be leaving in the morning. When she asked about her book, he told her it was gone. "You don't need a book," he said. "What you need is some good mountain air. I knew we should not have moved to this valley."

So up the high mountain they moved. Sacha had not spoken a word all night and day. She simply stared up at the sky where her mother lived.

Weeks went by and months, and still Sacha did not speak a word. At first Searcher thought it was because she was angry with him. Soon he realized something was terribly wrong.

Searcher sat by the little brook that wound past their new cave. He was worried to distraction.

"What should I do," he asked the sky. "You have taken my wife and now it seems you want my Sacha as well. All she does is stare up at you day and night."

The brook, which had been babbling away beside him,

now spoke with perfect clarity. "You are asking for answers you already know," it said. "You search for the treasure you yourself have buried."

"How would you know anything about me," he snarled.

"I am the water of life," it said. "I have tried every way there is to reach you. I have showered you with love, and you have shaken me off. I have bathed you in my grace, and you have wallowed in the mud of self-pity. When you had the chance to drink me in, you choked and spat me out in favor of being drunk with your own power to control me."

The water rose up in a tall column and then flattened out to become a sort of screen. Searcher saw his daughter and her mother lying in a field of wildflowers and laughing. It was a strange image because Sacha was the age she was now, not a cub, as when her mother had been with them. Then the two of them began to float up and away.

In a flash he realized what he was seeing. He leapt up and ran to the cave. Sacha sat outside it, her eyes closed and her face tilted up to the sky.

"Don't go," he cried to her. "Please, baby. Stay with Papa."

He heard the watery voice of the brook saying, "Things never stay the same. Better to change them yourself than to have them do you a mischief. Sacha is making her own change."

Searcher knew what he had to do. He scooped Sacha into his arms and ran with her to the brook. He waded in up to his waist and floated her on the surface. Lovingly he poured the cool water over her forehead and patted it over her eyes.

"I have come to you," he said to the waters of life. "I have brought Sacha with me. Wash us clean of this terrible fear and pain. I will teach her to swim in you and we will drink you in. I promise never to shake you off again. We will stay here. We will not ever move again, for I have everything I need here in my arms."

With those words Sacha stirred. She opened her eyes and focused on him. "I missed you," she said and smiled. "Have we found our happiness?"

Searcher cried with relief and joy at having his daughter back. Then he laughed and gave them both a dunking.

When they surfaced Sacha laughed. "Are we really staying here Papa," she asked. "Will I make real friends I can keep forever?"

"Yes my child," Searcher said. He took her hand and placed it on the surface of the water. "This is someone I want to introduce you to, a friend who will never leave you. One who will always listen, who is everywhere at once. Knowing this friend you will never be lonely again."

So his search ended when he found where he began.

Eagle's Flight to Heaven's Wall

In his nest on the high ledge of the cliffs sat the eagle. His sharp, clear eyes were locked on his objective. All his life he had known where he wanted to go and what he wanted to achieve.

"The top of the mountain," he said to his mate. "I will crest Heaven's Wall."

His mate wanted him to be happy. Despite the fact that she loved their home in the cliffs, overlooking the valley and the river, she would go where he led.

Every season they moved to a different nest, each one closer to the mountain. Each time they moved the air got thinner, and her mate was away more making his practice flights. She knew that he had to build his strength, speed and endurance for the steep flight to the top.

In the mornings, just as the dawn broke he would begin his hunt for the morning meal of fish from the river or small prey from the valley. Then he would leave her and begin his ascent up Heaven's Wall Mountain.

He was always so focused on his preparation and goal that he seldom remembered to give his mate a peck goodbye. When he returned to the nest he would flop down and fall asleep.

This season was the worst yet, since they were now within striking distance of the mountain and he would soon make his big flight.

"I can feel it," he said to his mate. "This is the day. The air currents are perfect. It is cool and mild, and the skies are clear. I will make the flight today."

He added, "I will beat the mountain today. Everyone will know how great I am."

Since she had never dared ask what would happen once the flight had actually been made, his mate was not sure how she felt about this. She worked up her courage and asked.

"Once you reach the top, what will happen?"

He was stunned. How could she ask such a foolish thing. Once he had made it to the top their lives would be perfect. He would be revered among all creatures for his prowess.

With a tinge of annoyance in his voice he said, "We shall be blissfully happy there. You will have everything you have ever dreamed of. I promise you that."

His mate had never had big dreams. She had wanted love and security and a mate with whom to share the great joys of life. She was sure she had all those things now, but if her mate said it, it must be true. Her trust in him was as boundless as her love.

Then a thought nagged at her. "If it has taken you all your life to become strong enough to fly to the top of the mountain, then how will I fly up to join you?"

"Don't be ridiculous. It is so like you to ruin my moment of triumph by worrying about yourself. All will be well once I have reached the summit," he said. "If you are so worried about it then perhaps you should fly half-way and then walk up the rest to meet me."

This seemed a very difficult task to his mate, but she did not wish to disappoint him.

"All right," she said. "I will do as you suggest. I will see you at the top."

So it was that the eagle set out on his flight with all his neighbors cheering his departure.

Meanwhile, his mate began her flight along a separate face of the mountain. She chose a different path at his encouragement. She thought he was being kind, showing her a safer route. In truth, he did not want her to steal his thunder. When he rose, he wanted all eyes to be on him.

Eagle knew every span of sky. He started out slowly and then gained speed as he used the wind to glide and soar up and up to the summit. He felt glorious. He was the all-powerful bird of the skies, and none could match him.

The higher he got the more his lungs burned from lack of oxygen. He had trained for this and was able to take shallow breaths and rise in wheeling circles on the updrafts.

Unfortunately, his mate had not the benefit of training, or advice, and so she barely made the mid-point without plummeting from the sky. Faint with exertion and the thin air, she rested on a ledge. She could just make out the shape of her mate as he rose on the other side of the sky. She was so proud.

"I must not disappoint him," she said to herself. Taking a ragged breath, she began to work her way up the sheer face of the mountain. She would inch her way along the tilted ledge and then fly up to the next level. Occasionally she could make longer flights and save her chipping talons from the harsh work of climbing.

As time wore on her strength began to flag. The sun shone brilliantly above the mountain and looking up was difficult. She closed her eyes and asked the mountain for help.

"Please," she said humbly. "I am not trying to climb you for myself. I do not want anything from you, but to survive and live happily with my mate. I am not here to conquer you. I know that you are greater than I. Only, please great one, allow me to rise, and I will tell everyone I meet how you gave me your strength and helped me on my way."

The mountain rumbled. Then a deep voice that seemed to come from all around her spoke. "I do not make deals, little one," it said. "If I help you to the top it is for my own reasons. They may not be reasons you can appreciate or accept."

The lady eagle knew that the mountain had all the power. It had but to shrug its massive shoulders to send her plummeting or to bury her in rock.

"What is it then that I should do," she asked. "Am I to die here, alone?"

The rock beneath her warmed and the ledge expanded to allow her to lie and rest. "Do you feel alone," the mountain asked.

"No," she said. "Now I feel fine."

"I will help you to the summit," the mountain said. "Once you are there, you must do as I wish. You must not claim credit for yourself. Trust that I will save you. Can you do these things."

She was not sure that she could and so, being a truthful bird, said, "I do not know if I am that strong. I will do my best."

So it was that the mountain shifted and made a moving stair of rock that the she rode to the top, arriving just in time to see her mate approach.

Half-dead with exhaustion he landed at her feet. She covered him with her wing and rocked him. It was such a relief to see him safe and whole. It took several minutes before he recovered himself and realized at whom he was looking.

"You," he screeched. "How is it possible? How could you?"

Flustered by this hostile greeting she offered him water. He dashed it away and attacked.

"No," she cried. "I tried to go up the mountain as you said but it was too difficult. It was the mountain itself that helped me make it here before you. I only conceded that it was more powerful and it brought me to the top."

He was blind with rage and humiliation. Such talk! Did she actually think he would believe her story about the mountain coming to life? She must have been training in secret. She had planned to steal his glory all along.

The eagle's rage knew no boundaries. He pecked at her

eyes and beat her with his massive wings. His talons tore at her heart.

Finally, as she lay at the edge of the abyss the mountain shook.

A wall of rock rose between the two birds. The male eagle fell back in terror. He realized that his mate had told the truth. "What have I done," he cried. "I am sorry. Please let me go to her."

The voice of the mountain was solemn and hard as granite. "You have placed yourself and your ego above all else in life eagle," it said. "Today you have sacrificed your love for your own betterment. What you are feeling now is fear, not regret."

It was true, but eagle would not admit it aloud.

"You are a hard one to teach eagle," the mountain said. "I will keep your wife with me until you can find your way. You have damaged your wings in your attack and they will not mend sufficiently for you to make this flight again. If you want to return to this place you must humble yourself before me."

Eagle panicked. He decided to lie to the mountain. He would say what it wanted to hear in order to get what he wanted.

"Anything you say," he shouted. "You are all powerful. I am nothing. I have learned my lesson."

The wall between the birds lowered, and he saw his mate bloodied and unmoving at the edge where the mountain met the sky. She was nodding her head as if agreeing with some instruction she was receiving, but he heard nothing.

She heard the voice of the rock beneath her say, "You have done well child. Now roll off the edge and I will save you."

Her mind was hazy with pain but she remembered her promise. With the last of her power, she rolled off the edge and fell cartwheeling through the air.

"No," cried her mate. But he was too late. Rushing to the edge he saw her falling.

Then the rock of the mountain reached out and enveloped her in mid-air. The rock retracted back into the body of the mountain and she vanished.

The mountain continued to shudder. Eagle looked down to see its face shifting and changing. The side of the mountain became smooth and polished as glass. Etched on the face of the polished rock was an image of his love in flight. It stretched for miles and could be seen far down in the valley.

"Don't take her, please," eagle begged and wept.

"You have given her to me," the mountain replied. "Now go back to the base and start over again. The day you are strong enough to ask me to help you rise to the summit, I will reunite you with your mate."

In the blink of an eye, eagle found himself standing in his empty nest and gazing at the mountain. He looked up at the image emblazoned across its face and wept.

He cried for his mate, but more for himself. For now he knew that he was not all-powerful. Unfortunately, it would be many years and many tears before his image would join that of his mate on the sheer face of Heaven's Wall.

BEGINNING
AGAIN

The Crane Stories

An old woman lived alone in a tiny pink house by the bay.

Although she had no children or family of her own to be with her, she was never lonely. She was a storyteller, and every day the children of the village would gather around her to listen.

The woman's name was Betty. Every afternoon, when the warm breeze blew across the bay, she and the children would sit under a palm tree and Betty would tell them her Crane stories.

Betty began the telling the same way every day: "When the days are long and my heart is sad I sit by the water and think. That is when the crane flies to me and tells me about his home in the sky."

Everyone in the village knew that the home of the crane was more beautiful than any place on earth. It was a place filled with a beautiful golden light all day and at night even the darkness was deep and rich and beautiful.

The crane could look down from his home and see every living thing, and he thought that everything he saw was worth visiting.

Using his great white wings the bird had flown all around the world and seen many things. Some were good and some made the crane very sad.

"I remember an evening when the crane came to visit and I could see that his feathers were wet from crying," Betty told. "When I asked why he was so sad he said he had seen people treating each other badly. In some places even they were fighting and hurting each other with words. Sometimes he saw them hurting with more than words."

This made some of the people hearing the story look away as they remembered unkind things they had said or done.

"Why does the crane visit you and not us," one child asked. "Does he think we are not worth visiting?"

"Well," Betty said. "Once, he told me that he visits everyone, but not everyone can see or hear him. Many people have seem him, but thought he was just another bird. Some have seen him and shooed him away. I think that eventually, everyone will see him when they are ready."

That made the children very excited. Many of them had already seen the bird fly past. Some even heard his voice. Unfortunately, many had never seen or heard him, and some were beginning to doubt that Betty had really seen him.

Betty thought awhile longer and added, "I think maybe, he likes having me tell you all about him, and so he helps me see him a bit more clearly to make the telling easier."

When one of the children asked the name of the crane, Betty said, "He has no name. He told me that if he allowed one person to give him a name then people would believe he belonged only to that person. Since he wants to belong to everyone, he decided it would be better not to have a name."

Betty went on telling her stories for many more years. The children at her telling tree grew up and had children of their own who came to listen.

One day she was so old and so tired that she could not get up from her bed. Her heart was sad because she could not get up to tell her stories or even sit by the water to wait for the crane.

She lay in bed and began to cry. Suddenly she heard a tapping at her bedside window. She reached over and opened the window. In flew the bird.

"Oh, my friend," Betty said. "I was too tired to look for you."

The bird was looking especially large and white. "You do not have to worry," he said. "You found me a long time ago, and now it is time for me to find you and bring you home with me."

"Oh, but I can't leave my village," Betty cried. "Who will tell the children about you?"

The crane stretched his great wing out over her bed, but instead of a shadow, cast a golden light.

"Do not worry old friend," he said. "I will find someone to visit here when you have flown with me. I promise the stories will continue as long as there are children to listen."

The Gardener

A man planted a garden and he filled it with dozens of flowering plants and trees.

There were dogwood trees and cherry trees, sprays of wisteria, rows of daffodils and mountains of azaleas. The garden was a riot of color and fragrance; still the man was disappointed year after year because the one tree he wanted to see flower produced buds and no more.

For months the man labored, hauling fertilizer, pruning the branches, mulching the base. He spoke to the tree and watered it lovingly.

While he cared for the rest of the garden he could never sit back and enjoy it because his anticipation of the great tree was too powerful.

His unhappiness did not go unnoticed among the plants he tended.

The rhododendron with its brilliant purple blooms shed petal tears when the man only gave it a cursory nod.

The bluebells clanged in discord when he yanked the weeds, but failed to stop and admire them. The roses lifted their faces so that he might inhale their heady fragrance as he passed, but he only muttered about killing the aphids he spotted on their leaves.

"This has to stop," cried the garden gnome that lay on its side after the man had stubbed his toe on it and thus kicked it over. "What is that silly tree he goes on and on about? I have never heard him speak its name."

A voice croaked from the toad abode in the shadow of a birch, "That is the If Only tree to which he tends."

"Oh dear," said the weeping willow and began to cry fresh tears. "Not one of those. They're always a disappointment."

The If Only tree was known to everyone in the garden as the one plant that took all a gardener had to give and never bloomed in return.

It was said that if a gardener fed it his hopes, his dreams and his fears it would give him his heart's desire some day. But while the tree grew to enormous height and girth its buds withered on the branches. The danger was great. It would inevitably wear the gardener down, and when he stopped doting on it the tree would leech the life from the rest of the garden. All would wither and die.

The garden fell silent as the man returned to sit on the marble bench by his favorite tree. He sat by it for hours and spoke and spoke, and none had listened before today. Now they all perked up and strained to hear his words.

"If only I had a bigger house," he told the tree, "Then I could be happy. If only I had a better car I could take my children to the zoo or to visit the relatives."

Then the gardener's wife came into the garden and sat beside her husband and spoke to the tree. "If only I were thin, then I would be happy. If only I were beautiful, then I would have friends."

When the couple left the garden the tree grew another inch, and the shadow it cast over the garden made the other plants shiver.

"We have to nip this in the bud," barked the dogwood.

"To late for that," snapped the snapdragon

It was Lilly who intervened with a plan to save the garden.

"We must talk to the wind," she said. "We must ask it to bring a terrible storm and strike the tree and down it with a bolt of lightening."

The garden was aghast. A storm of that magnitude would surely wipe them out.

"True," said Lilly. "The storm would likely do us damage, but the If Only will surely kill the garden as well."

So it was done, and the plants asked the wind to rage, and it did. The garden was decimated. Flowers and trees were strewn in every direction, but to their horror, the If Only tree stood tall as ever.

The man entered the garden and wept. Looking at the ruin, he pictured his beautiful garden. He knew that, while he had tended it, he had not appreciated it. "If Only . . ." he sighed.

The tree shook with laughter. The man jumped back in shock.

"Such a foolish man," it laughed. "You still have me."

Then the man heard a small, silvery voice. Lilly, who

lay at the base of its trunk, said, "Root it out. It's your only chance. All of the beauty and glory you once sowed will grow back once the If Only tree is dead and gone."

The man knew she was right, but the tree suddenly seemed so large that he doubted he could do the job. It was too much work and he was tired and sick at heart.

"Get your wife to come and help you. Call a friend, a brother and neighbor to help you," Lilly pleaded.

"The man shrugged, "That would be too humiliating," he said.

Another voice called from a tangle of plants; the gnome shouted, "More humiliating than being dictated to by a malignant growth? Come on man, show some spunk. You put your back into building things, growing things, pulling the little weeds so that the garden would grow. Now you have to pull the big one so that it can be revived."

Other small voices of the bulbs he had planted called out to him from beneath the soil, "We will come back to you. You must be strong."

So he swallowed his pride and went to fetch his wife and his neighbors and between them they chopped down the If Only tree and dug out the stump and burned it on a great pyre.

The next year the man, his wife, his neighbors and friends all gathered in the garden, among the new sprigs and blooms to erect a sundial where the If Only tree had once stood.

They placed it there to remind them that shadows pass, and with time all can be green again.

Phoenix Rising

hoenix lived in a canyon of orange rock at the end of the desert.

He was a tough old bird. In his mind, life had always been cruel to him. His lovers had turned on him. His wealth had never materialized and every day was a new insult.

When the sun rose and shone across the arid terrain the bird was taken with a fit of pique.

"The sun shines to mock me," he cried. "It blinds me and bakes me and dries away the water. It drives away all other life and I have no companionship."

A scorpion scuttling across the bird's path paused to listen.

"Stand in the shade of the cliffs," the spiny one said. "Drink from the springs in the caves. Also, saying 'Good morning' once in a while would be a nice change of pace."

The phoenix became so enraged that it burst into flames and fell to dust. A few moments later it rose again. "You are another curse on me," the bird spat. "You only tell me these things to anger me to the point of self destruction."

The scorpion looked up at the bird; "I have never seen such a waste of talent in all my life."

"How dare you insult me," the bird raged.

The scorpion leapt upon the bird and stung it, until again the bird burst into flames of rage and fell to dust. Again the bird rose and stalked toward the scorpion.

"Why did you do that," it screeched.

"Oh just a lesson to show how your anger hurts you more than it does me," the scorpion said casually. The bird was beside itself with anger and confusion.

"Can't you see what a horrible life the creator of all things has given me," the bird demanded. "I have been cursed to die a thousand deaths. There is no worse fate!"

"None greater," countered the scorpion. "I would gladly change places."

"What do you mean you poisonous insect," demanded the bird.

The scorpion said, "I am filled with poison, but so are you. My poison kills, but once. From yours you yourself die a thousand deaths."

He went on, "You have a soul filled with anger and hatred for all things. Yet the creator of all things has given you eternal life. You think his gift a curse. It is not."

The bird was dumbfounded.

"Your power to regenerate was not given so that you could survive self-destruction," scorpion said. "You could die for your beliefs and rise again. You could give love to the world until you fall to ashes and then rise again to greater acts of glory. What a gift!"

For a moment all was silent. Phoenix spread his wings and flew straight up into the clear blue sky.

As if for the first time he saw the colors of the earth below. He heard the hum of insects, felt the thrill of the wind.

A great cry emerged from the bird. "Forgive me," he called up to the heavens.

Phoenix exploded like a firework, raining down over the sands, then rose from the desert floor.

Scorpion asked, "Have you seen the light?"

"Yes," the bird said softly. "It glows from every grain of sand in this desert."

"What desert," asked the scorpion.

The bird looked around and saw lush green fields. The scorpion was gone and in its place sat a small gray dove.

"Where did the scorpion go," the phoenix asked.

The bird stretched its wings. "I am here. The desert is here too, beneath the meadow. It is all in the way you choose to view it. You have simply chosen a new way."

"Will I ever go back to the desert," the phoenix asked in distress.

His companion shrugged. "Every day you choose where you awake. Will it be the desert or the meadow? You will choose the way you see your fellows—scorpions or doves."

"But I only want to live in the meadow with the doves," worried the phoenix.

The dove smiled, "Then by all means, do."

Mallard Takes the Cake

akota was the kind of creature that other animals flocked to. This was especially surprising because she was a skunk.

Now by most folks' standards a skunk is the sort of furry animal that should be given a wide berth. Nobody likes to go around smelling like old cheese and dirty socks, as is usually the result of a close encounter with one of the skunk set.

In truth, Dakota had done her share of accidentally altering the scent of some of her neighbors. There were bound to be times when someone, though well meaning, would take her by surprise and get treated to a stink bomb.

The difference between Dakota and other skunks was her sense of humor and of course her very impressive way of apologizing. Whenever she was forced to use her defenses she would always regret it. She would make up for it by baking a very grand spice cake for the unfortunate victim.

It so happened that Dakota had a best friend, Mallory Mallard. The two would spend long hours, telling jokes and stories and gossiping about this and that. One of their favorite stories was about the time Mallory was drying off after a swim and made such a big racket in the reeds that she terrified Dakota into making her stink for a week.

"I forgave you," she said. "I knew it was just an accident."

Dakota smiled. "Yes indeed, though I seem to recall having to bake you two spice cakes that time." Both laughed until their sides ached.

One day, an old and dear friend of Mallory's was visiting from a distant pond. Mallory was so excited about her old friend's visit that she completely forgot to meet Dakota at their usual spot for lunch and chat.

By the time she realized her mistake it was too late in the day to call on Dakota. The next day she apologized profusely. "Oh I am so sorry," she quacked. "I just don't know where my head was, or my manners."

Although she was a little hurt by her friend's forgetfulness she forgave her. "Don't give it another thought," she said. "We will meet tomorrow at our usual spot and this will be just a funny memory. We shall call it The Great Day of Forgetting. You forgot our meeting and now I shall forget to be cross."

So it was agreed that they would meet the next day.

In the morning Mallory packed a lunch and headed off toward the pond. Dakota also packed a lunch and headed to the appointed spot.

Just as they stepped up to the mossy bank there was a terrible crashing in the reeds and something burst out at them. Mallory jumped back just as Dakota let fly with a great cloud of stench that enveloped the invader.

"Take that," squeaked Dakota. "You beast! Sneak attacker! You dangerous fiend."

When the dust settled and the cloud dispersed, Mallory gasped in horror. Lying on the ground was her old and dear friend, Hattie Pheasant. Her long tail feathers had fallen out in the attack and her eyes were swollen shut from the cloud of toxic gas.

"Oh Dakota how could you? This is my old and dear friend you have hurt," she cried. "Why, I believe you knew who it was all along. You did this on purpose just to get back at me. You hurt an innocent creature. I shall never speak to you again."

Dakota didn't know what to do. "I was protecting you," she said. "All that noise made me think it was a big cat or even a wolf. I was trying to save you. Please forgive me."

"Never," Mallory said.

The two birds waddled off leaving Dakota to cry out her sorrows.

The next day Dakota baked two spice cakes and brought them to Mallory's nest. The duck only hissed at her and told her to leave.

"The nerve of her thinking she could buy my forgiveness with a cake," Mallory huffed to Hattie. "I shall never forgive her. Never. She is a menace to society."

Hattie, who had long since recovered and after several baths in tomato juice, no longer smelled badly, was not so angry.

"Now dearie, she didn't mean to do it," Hattie said with a chuckle. "I am over it. Surely you can forgive her.

After all, it was not you who had to sit in a tub of tomatoes all night long."

Mallory would not hear of it. "Hurting my friend hurts me. She did it on purpose. I am so embarrassed by her behavior. I shall never speak to her again."

Now Hattie was a very smart bird. She knew that Mallory loved her and that she and Dakota had been friends only a little while. She appreciated the loyalty, but knew that shutting her new friend out of her life would take a terrible toll on Mallory. She did not want to see that happen.

"My dear, dear, old friend," Hattie soothed. "Have you not forgiven Dakota in the past? Have other animals not done you far more harm only to be forgiven by you?"

Mallory thought about this. "Well, yes. But those times were different."

"How so," Hattie asked.

"Well those wrongs were done to me," she said.

Hattie nodded wisely. "Yes, it is always easier to forgive someone for harming you than one you love," she said. "I have known this to be the case in my own life. Why do you suppose that is?"

"Because I always put others needs above my own. So I was taught by all the learned birds, that the creator of all animals would want it that way," she answered. "You are more important than I."

Hattie shook her feathered head. Her friend had a good heart, but did not always use it in conjunction with her head.

"I will not pretend to know the mind of the great creator

of all birds, but I will tell you that we are all important," Hattie said. "You must love yourself as you love me. Then you must learn really to forgive. When you forgave Dakota for hurting you it meant little because you did not place any value on yourself, so you never really learned to forgive. You only learned to forget."

Mallory was struck to the core by these words. She didn't know whether to cry in protest or in sorrow. She chose sorrow. Sorrow for herself and for Dakota.

"Excuse me please my old and wise friend," Mallory sniffed. "I have to go see a friend."

"I thought that might turn out to be the case," Hattie said.

Mallory found Dakota sitting by the reeds next to the pond. In a very loud voice she called to her, "It is Mallory. I am approaching from behind you. I say this so you will not be surprised, though I would not blame you if you made me smell for a month. My behavior was rotten enough to match any smell you can send my way."

Dakota gave a little hiccup of a laugh. "I am very glad to hear you say that," she said. "Have you really forgiven me?"

Mallory took Dakota under her wing, "I have done better than that. I have forgiven us both. What do you say to starting over again?"

Dakota smiled, "Wonderful. Since we both needed forgiveness, does that mean we each must bake a cake?"

Mallory quacked with glee, "Well it would certainly be better than eating my own words again."

Then she added, "Let us not buy forgiveness, nor shall we expect gifts to salve our bruised feelings. The cakes will taste sweeter if they are not filled with the fruit of guilt or iced with the bitterness of remorse."

The Painter and the Fox

ach morning Art arose in darkness. He would fumble around his small studio, find the matches and light a candle.

Then he would look directly into the flame and clear his mind of all thoughts. That is when the colors would come into his mind.

Quickly, he snatched up his brushes and paints and set to work on the broad canvas that was the sky. Art was a sunrise painter, hired by the universe to decorate the mornings of all time.

Some mornings he would look into the flame and see just a few muted strains of rose and gold feathering their way up from the horizon. Other times he would see miles of umber, yellows and bold reds. Some times it would come out all in silvery white with just a hint of pale gold.

Art loved painting the sunrise for it gave him great satisfaction to start everyone's day off in beauty. It also gave him his days and evenings free.

On one particularly bright and colorful morning Art was sitting on the grass and enjoying the fruits of his labors.

"Nice one," said a sharp voice at his elbow. It was the fox. His pointy countenance was creased with a sly smile.

He looked Art up and down. "It's a shame that you give us such beautiful sunrises while the sunsets have been so terribly drab of late."

Had they? Art had not noticed any lack of flair in the fading of the light that came at day's end.

"You know," continued the Fox, "I heard that you were due for a promotion. The universe is humming your name my boy. Everyone loves your work."

Art, a fellow of few words, only smiled. It was good to know that he had pleased so many.

"Of course I realize that you have a problem," Fox said. "You are only one person and painting both sunrise and sunset is perhaps more than you can handle alone. What you need is an assistant. Someone to get out there and beat the bushes for new ideas. Let you know what the people really want to see in their light."

This sparked Art's interest. "What people want?" he asked. "I don't understand. I just look into my candle and see the colors that I am to paint."

Fox barked with laughter. This boy really was a babe in the woods. It was a wonder that he had managed to secure any position at all.

"My boy, my dear, dear boy," Fox said. "Let me take you in hand. Just sign this paper here and I will become your manager and assistant. Together we will rule the world."

Art did not wish to rule anything. All he needed was his work and the satisfaction of a job well done. Still, Fox seemed to know a great deal about life and the universe.

Art had never considered what people might want. Perhaps there were people he was displeasing. That would be terrible.

So it was that Art signed his deal with Fox and became the painter of both sunrise and sunset.

It was a heady time for the young man. He worked nearly around the clock. He barely took time to eat or sleep.

Fox did just as he had proposed and came to him with many new ideas. "Bolder colors," Fox suggested. "More contrast."

"Green," Fox insisted one day. "You never use green or black. Now that would really be new. Go on my boy. Use this new pallet I have brought you and these new electric lights. The florescent bulbs give off the most pleasant hum."

As time wore on, Art's work began to look jagged and stark. It took on an edge. Art himself began to change. Dark circles appeared beneath his eyes, his hair grew long and wild and his thin body became rangy and crooked.

Everyone noticed the changes in the sky. At first they liked what they saw. The change was a novelty. It was not long, however, before everyone began to clamor for the old softness, grandeur and simple beauty that had gone missing.

They chanted, and shouted and sent up planes to sky write their message of discontent. Now his work was not only ugly but covered with graffiti as well.

Fox had a keen sense of smell. He knew the sweet scent of success and also the sour odor of failure. He began to turn up his nose at Art.

"Well boy it is time we part company," he told Art one afternoon. "I have done all I can for you. Unfortunately, you have burnt your candle at both ends and are nothing but a nasty puddle of wax yourself. So long." Fox was gone in a blink.

Art looked up at the sky in sadness. It was dark and polluted and ugly. He had made a mess of things and was in despair. He put his head down and cried himself to sleep.

In his dreams he saw a beautiful light glimmering far off across a dark sea. He was in a little boat and paddling with all his might toward it. No matter how hard he paddled, he made no headway.

"Stop paddling," said a voice in his ear.

"I can't stop," he said breathlessly. "I will never get anywhere that way."

"Stop paddling and cast away your oars," the voice said. "See what happens."

Deciding that nothing could be worse than drifting in the darkness, Art tossed away the oars and watched them float off.

"Now look at me, for I am the light in the distance," said the voice. "Keep your eyes on me."

Art listened and obeyed the voice and suddenly the boat began to move; slowly at first and then at a good clip. The sky grew lighter and lighter until Art was moving along the wide blue waters under a blue sky. The salty air cleared his head and the warmth of the sun sank into him and seemed to heal his tired body.

"Now awake. Light your candle and begin the day," said the voice. "From now on listen only to my voice. See only my light and follow where my current takes you. Then will you find your work pure and beautiful again."

Art awoke in the darkness. Laid his hand unerringly on the book of matches. Lit his candle and painted a sunrise more glorious than any the universe had ever seen.

The Faith Healer

here was a boy who was very friendly. He said hello to everyone he met and gave the gift of a smile.

One day, an old man was walking past the boy's yard. The man looked tired and asked the boy if he could take a rest on his front steps.

The boy smiled and invited the man to sit.

Knowing he was not allowed to talk to strangers, the boy excused himself and went to fetch his mother to meet the man.

The mother greeted the man and brought him some milk and fresh bread.

The man told them of how he had once been very poor but that he had become rich when given a special gift of a candle.

"When the candle is lit," he said, "Your hopes are answered."

This seemed strange to the boy because the man was not dressed in fancy clothes and he was walking instead of driving a fancy car.

Since the boy was taught always to be polite to his elders he did not argue with the man. He had never heard of believing or wishing or hopes before, but he was very interested in the man's story.

When the man was rested he thanked the boy and his mother and went on with his walk.

A few days later the boy went out to play and found a small box on the steps. It had a card that said, "Light me, believe and you will have all you need."

The boy was very excited. He took the box to his mother. Inside they found a beautiful glass ball, the size of a baseball.

It was clear glass with red stripes flowing down it from top to bottom. It looked like a large, clear peppermint. It was filled with oil and had a wick. It was a glass oil candle.

"Shall we light it?" his mother asked.

The boy thought for a moment and then said yes.

Lighting the candle the boy's mother asked, "What will you hope for?"

The boy thought very hard. Since they had been very poor for a long time they had very little furniture in their house. The boy did not have a bed, only a mattress to sleep on.

"I would hope we get some furniture soon," he said.

The candle was lit.

Every day the boy lit the candle with his mother. They sat together staring at the beautiful little flame and thought about how nice it would be to have beds, tables, chairs and the like for their little house.

A week went by and nothing happened. Still they lit the candle.

Then one day a woman knocked at the door. "Hello, I am your new neighbor," she said. "We just moved in down the way and our house came with a lot of extra furniture. I was wondering if you could use some beds?"

Surprised, the boy got his mother, and together they carried home the new bed.

The next day a man knocked at the door. "Hello," he said. "I was just having a garage sale and there is a lot of furniture leftover. I am going around to the neighbors to see who would like a table and some chairs."

So it went. Day after day for nearly a month, strangers of all kinds stopped at the little house bringing everything from dishes to pictures, fish tanks, garden rakes, lamps and odd bits of things.

Often, people brought things that the boy and his mother did not really need or even like, but they were very polite and didn't like to refuse an offer of kindness. They knew that giving made people feel good, and they didn't want their neighbors to feel bad.

One afternoon the old man stopped by the house and waved to the boy.

The child could hardly wait to tell him about the miraculous candle and to thank him.

"It's amazing," said the boy. "But we have too much now. How do we turn it off?"

The man laughed and laughed. "I am sorry my child," he said. "It was your faith that brought about the giving miracle and you don't want to shut that off. Share your new wealth and your faith, and all will be well."

So the boy and his mother set about sharing their new possessions with their neighbors. They told of how their believing had brought about the Giving Miracle.

Word spread of the miraculous candle and how it had brought them riches.

Unfortunately, one night a burglar who had heard of the candle broke into the little house and stole the candle away. In the morning the mother saw that the candle was stolen, and began to cry. The boy too began to cry.

There was a knock at the door. It was the old man. "Why are you crying," he asked the boy.

"Because the wonderful candle has been stolen away," he sobbed. "Now we cannot make any more wishes, and we cannot help our neighbors."

The old man smiled and patted the boy on the head and dried his tears.

"Only the glass and oil were stolen," he explained. "Those things cannot give or receive. It was your faith that brought your good fortune, and it was your kind heart that helped you to give to your neighbors."

He added, "Believing is a strange thing. You can throw your faith away, but it can never be taken from you if you are not willing to let it go."

As he turned to go the boy cried out, "What is your name?"

"People call me the Faith Healer. That seems to do," he said and walked away down the road to another little house in the distance.

The Ride of Your Life

he pipe music floated on the salty wind drawing children to it like a magnet. It drew them all, but one.

Jo came daily to watch the magic of the carousel, but was not drawn by the sound. It was the fantasy of the carousel that attracted her. For it was a sad thing indeed, but Jo could not hear the music.

It was not a physical defect. Her ears felt the vibration that came from the wind that rushed through the majestic brass pipes of the calliope. Unfortunately, she had refused to hear the sounds of the world. She was afraid of people and the sounds they made.

They always seemed to sound angry as her parents did when they fought and shouted. So Jo had stopped listening and so had stopped hearing.

But her heart, now that was a different matter entirely. Her heart felt the movement of the carousel's magic. The feeling said the carousel was more than just the wood and paint that others saw.

To Jo, the wonder and marvel of the intricately carved figures of fancy with their gay colors and jeweled eyes was more fantastic than all the penny candy in the shop her parents owned.

In fact, since she had little pocket money to spend, Jo would take herself to the park where these creatures did their circle dance and simply sit and gaze at them.

Some moved up and down on their golden poles; others simply made a stately journey around the ring. All were her secret friends. She spoke to them in her own special language. What nobody knew was that they spoke back.

Every day of the summer Jo sat and watched the horses with their flying manes. There was Charger, all covered in armor; Dapple Gray and Rosie, so named for the wreath of flowers carved to hang around her neck. Her favorite was not a horse at all, but the one and only dragon with his swirling scaly tail.

Dragon held her heart because, being different from all the rest, most of the children were afraid to ride him. Some were even afraid to touch or walk past the scaly creature for fear that he might come to life and strike them.

A look, a nod and a flutter of her hands and the great aquamarine dragon would respond with a subtle change of pattern in his scales.

"So silly," Jo signed to Dragon as a little girl squealed and ran to her father after seeing he was not a pretty horse. "You are special, so strong and proud. I want to be just like you when I grow up."

Dragon patterned back, "You are already too much like me little one. I see you here every day, all alone. You speak to none but the carousel creatures. You are living in a circle just as I do. You must break out and join the world. I wish I could be like you."

Jo shook her head. "Silly Dragon, I cannot join the world, for I am too different. When I speak nobody hears me. When they speak I do not hear them. I belong here with you. I even have a plan for joining you forever."

Dragon was alarmed. Had she learned of the carousel's power to grant wishes? Had she grown big enough to reach the brass wishing rings that stuck out high above their heads? He dearly hoped she had not. Reaching for the rings was a dangerous business. Many fell. Those who did get their heart's desire were often disappointed by what they received.

"What is your plan little one," he asked.

Jo fixed her gaze far above Dragon's head, and he could see that she had indeed learned of the rings.

"You are too young yet," he said. "You cannot attempt that great a stretch."

Her eyes clouded with tears. She wanted so badly to be a carousel dragon. Once she was made of wood and paint and jewels she was sure she would no longer feel life's pain.

"Help me then," she signed. "Let me ride on your back and lift me so that I can reach for the wishing ring."

Because the old Dragon loved the little girl dearly he wanted her to be happy, and so he conceded to let her ride on his shoulder to grasp the ring.

"Don't you dare do it Dragon," Charger shouted from behind him. "It is a mistake. A bad battle plan indeed."

Rosie whinnied her agreement with Charger. "She is a child," she said. "She cannot know what is best for her. Stop immediately."

It was Dapple Gray who intervened. "You cannot force someone to see the right or wrong of a thing," he said. "The child must learn for herself if she if to survive in her world or in ours. Let her try."

So it was that on a bright sunny morning by the seaside a little girl paid her money and took her chances. She did not have to fight with the other children to get her place on Dragon, for none wanted to ride his scaly back.

The music began and the sun flashed on the mirrors that decorated the carousel's core. Jo carefully climbed to the top of Dragon's shoulder and made her reach for the ring. At the critical moment Dragon stretched and she felt the cool brass ring slip free from its holder and fall into her palm. It was much heavier than she had imagined it would be.

"I wish I were a dragon on the carousel," she wished.

The wind came up and the sun seemed to blind her for a moment. When she opened her eyes she could see her reflection in one of the mirrors. It had worked. Jo was a beautiful pink dragon with shining emeralds for eyes.

She wanted to jump for joy, but to her dismay she found that she could not move at all. She was stiff and hard all over. Something else was different. She could hear the music of the carousel. It was loud and it frightened her at first.

"What is wrong with me," she cried to Dragon. "I feel so cold and hard and I cannot move. Everything is loud and the world is spinning around me. I want to get off. Help me."

Dragon would have held her if he could, but being made of wood he could only think his thoughts to her.

"Do not panic," he said. "I was frightened too when I first became a carousel creature. We all were, but now we are accustomed to the spin and noise."

She did not understand. "Were you not always a wooden creature," Jo asked.

"No," he said. "I was once a man. I frightened people away with my harsh ways because I was afraid to care for others. I came here because I wanted to be a creature that nobody would ever bother with."

"Oh no dear," said Rosie. "I was a fine lady who lived in a big house. I was always running around in circles. Nothing was ever good enough for me. I always needed more and more until one day I came to the carousel and made my wish. I wished to always be a winner. So I became the horse with the prize of roses around my neck. Now I can never lose for I always stay exactly the same."

Charger spoke next, "I was a great warrior. I fought in many battles, until I realized that there were no battles left to fight. So I came here as an old man and wished to always be young and proud. Now I am the charger."

"What about you Gray," she asked. "Who were you?"

"I was nobody," he said. "I lived my life with no color or flair. I took life's ups and downs and felt nothing for anyone. I came here and asked to be where I could always watch life and never be a part of it."

Jo began to see things more clearly. She saw all the happy children waiting for their ride on the carousel. She also saw some adults bustling beside them. Some looked tired and irritated at having to ride the ride. Others were elated at the prospect of recalling their youth with a ride on the circle. One or two had that unhappy look of someone who wanted to wish their lives away.

Suddenly Jo knew that she did not want to wish hers away. She wanted to be a little girl again. Her pink claw still held the brass ring and so she took a chance and made a second wish.

"Please let me be alive again," she prayed. "I promise I will join the others this time. I will listen and I will hear."

The wind stirred and the sun flashed in the mirrors and Jo found herself sitting on Dragon's back. A kind man with white hair came over and patted her on the shoulder.

"Looks like you dozed off there for a minute," he said. "That's pretty dangerous. Maybe you'd better get off the ride."

Jo blinked and shook her head. The man had not signed to her. She had heard him, just as she had heard the music when she was a part of the carousel. She looked down at Dragon and saw that he had no life in him now. He did not make any change of pattern at all.

"You feeling well?" the man asked.

Jo found her voice for the first time. "I am fine," she said. "I just had a funny dream."

The man nodded in a very knowing way. "How about I buy you an ice cream and you can tell me all about it," he said. "My name is Draco. I think we are going to be good friends."

The horses on the carousel all watched as the two walked away.

"I'm going to miss him," sniffed Rosie.

"We should all be so lucky as the two of them," said Gray. "It is a rare thing to find a friend who can make the carousel magic work twice. Let's hope that some day we will find the friend who can free our spirits."